SPECIAL RECOMMENDATION FOR PAINTINGS BY YOUNG ARTISTS
JULIA RUAN

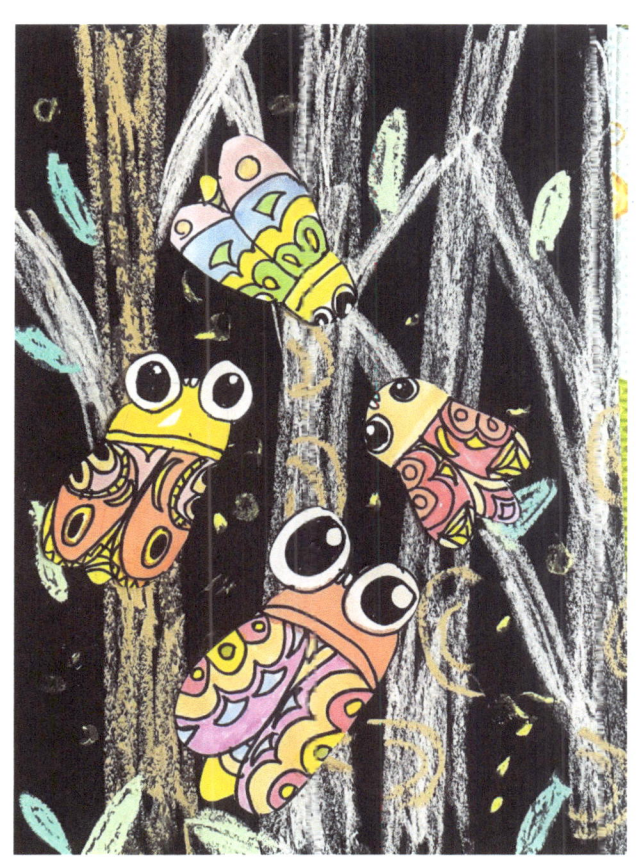

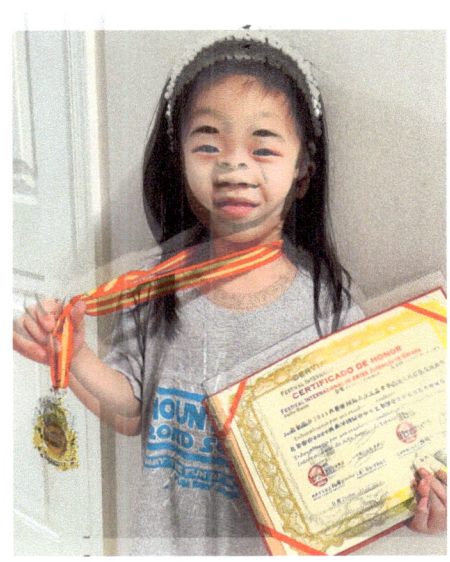

Julia Ruan is a smart and kind third-grade student who is eight years old. Just like most kids her age, she's energetic, loves to play with her friends, and has a passion for art.

Julia started out using her fingers, palms, and even her feet and face to create art. Later, she began using cotton swabs, Qtips, and eventually moved on to using crayons, pencils, markers, and other different types of drawing tools. Her early drawings lacked technique and appeared messy, but they showed her valuable and boundless imagination and creativity as a child.

After starting kindergarten, Julia loved visiting museums and was curious about everything, especially art museums. On weekends, her family would often take her to various museums and botanical gardens to explore exhibitions, observe flowers, and touch and feel everything. They hope these experiences allowed her to discover the beauty of the world and inspire her imagination.

Julia's biggest hobbies are drawing and reading. She's a very outgoing child, but whenever she's given a piece of paper and a pen to draw, her world immediately becomes peaceful. She likes to express herself through her drawings, using her pen to convey the message she wants to communicate. No matter what kind of mood or emotion she's feeling, it can be reflected in her artwork.

In 2020, Julia participated in the Ice and Snow Art Competition and won first place in the preschool group. She also entered the Hans Christian Andersen International Art Competition. This art piece won the junior group bronze award and has been selected for an international art exhibition at the Denmark Odense Hans Christian Andersen Museum.

Julia won a gold medal in First Sunflower National Children's Fine Art Competition in 2021. She also participated in the MOSTRA DIANO ART Competition and won the second prize.

In 2022, Julia participated in the Global Huaxia Cup competition, won the top award in her age group in this competition.

As of 2023, her love for painting has only grown stronger, and she is fortunate to have the opportunity to study with artist Weitao Yang. Under Mr. Yang's tutelage, she has learned many new painting techniques that have allowed her to push the boundaries of her artistry. We all hope that Julia will keep her passion for art and creation alive and to continue using her brush to record the small moments that make up the larger picture of life. In this way, she can witness the growth and beauty that life has to offer.

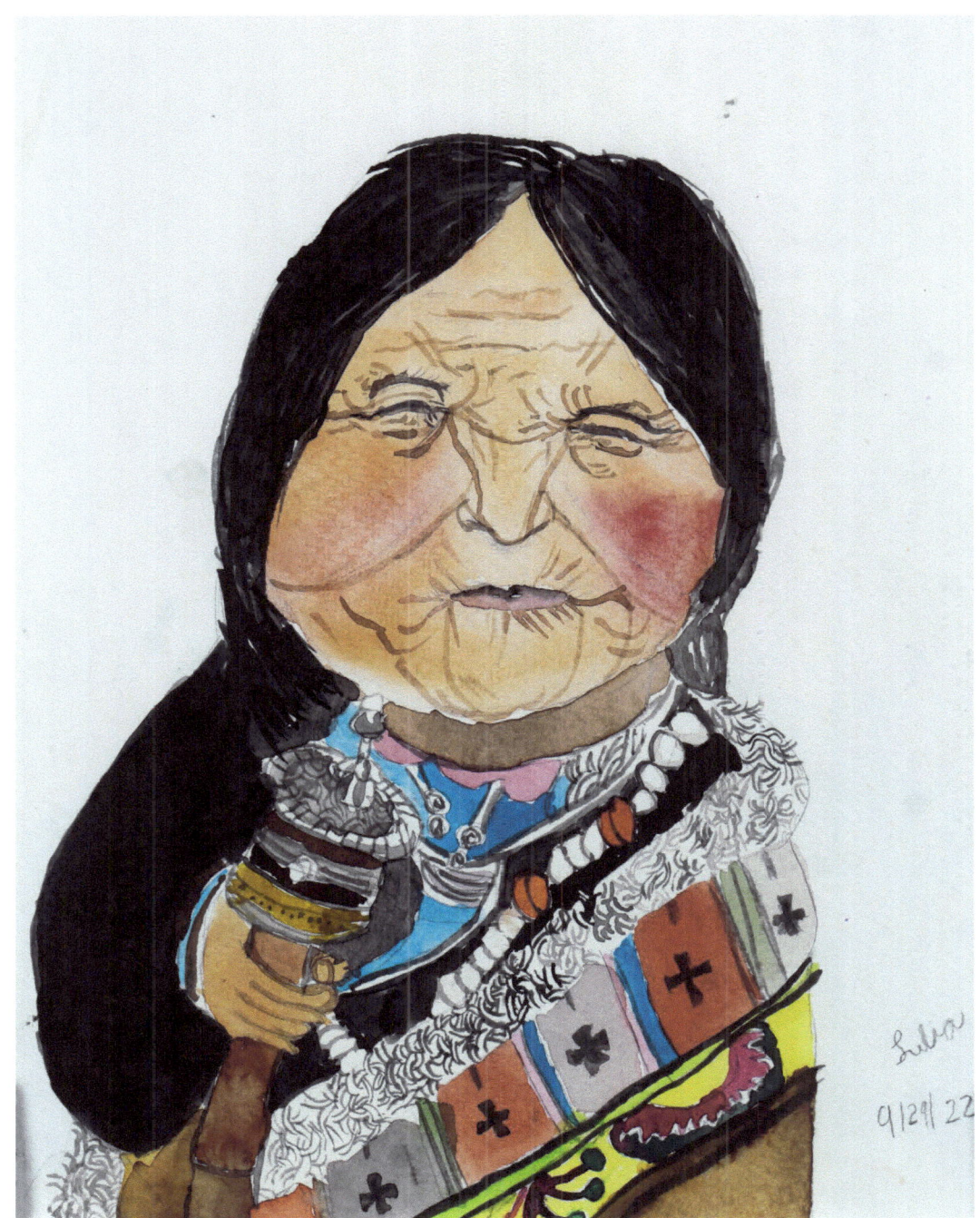

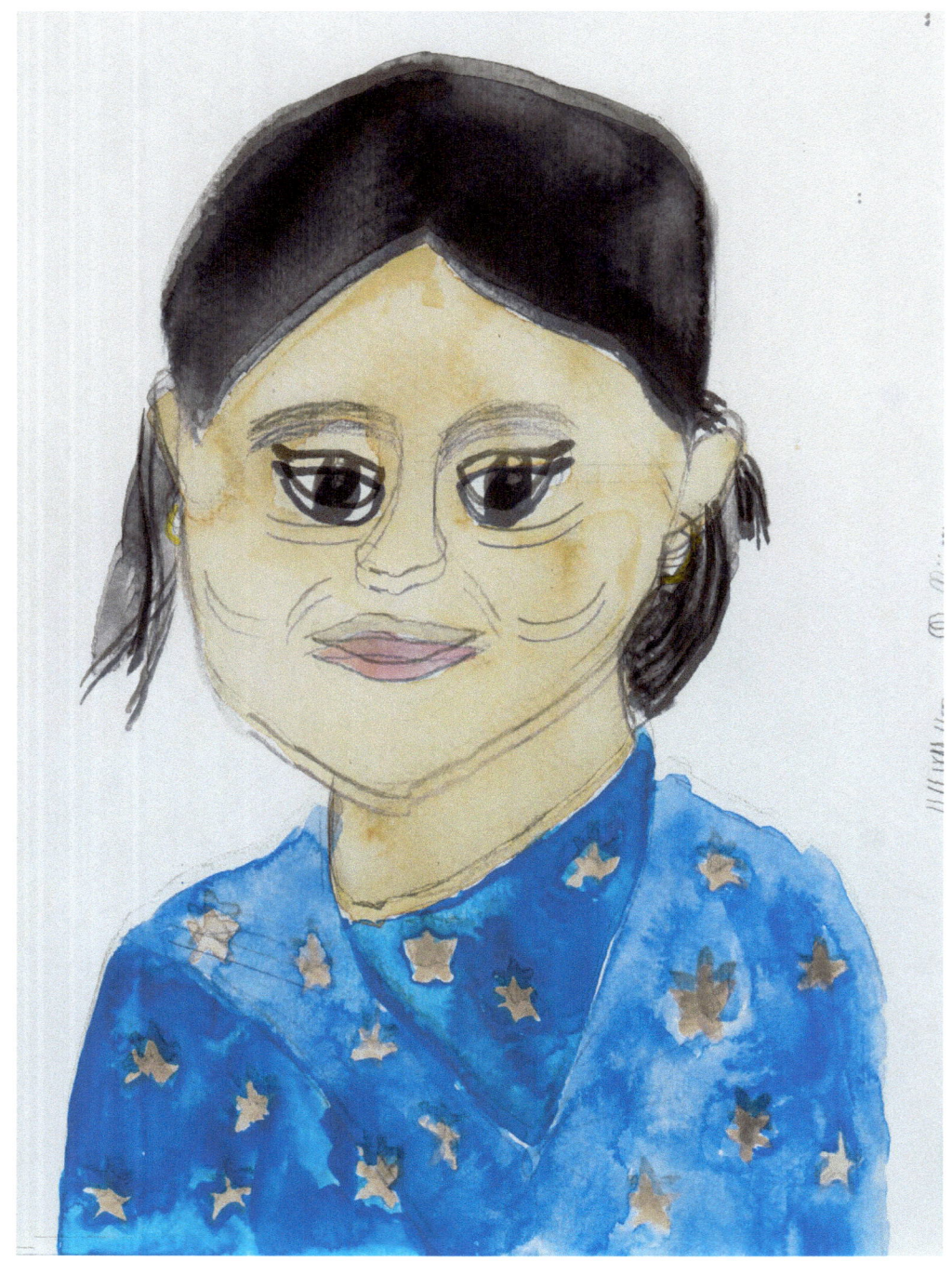

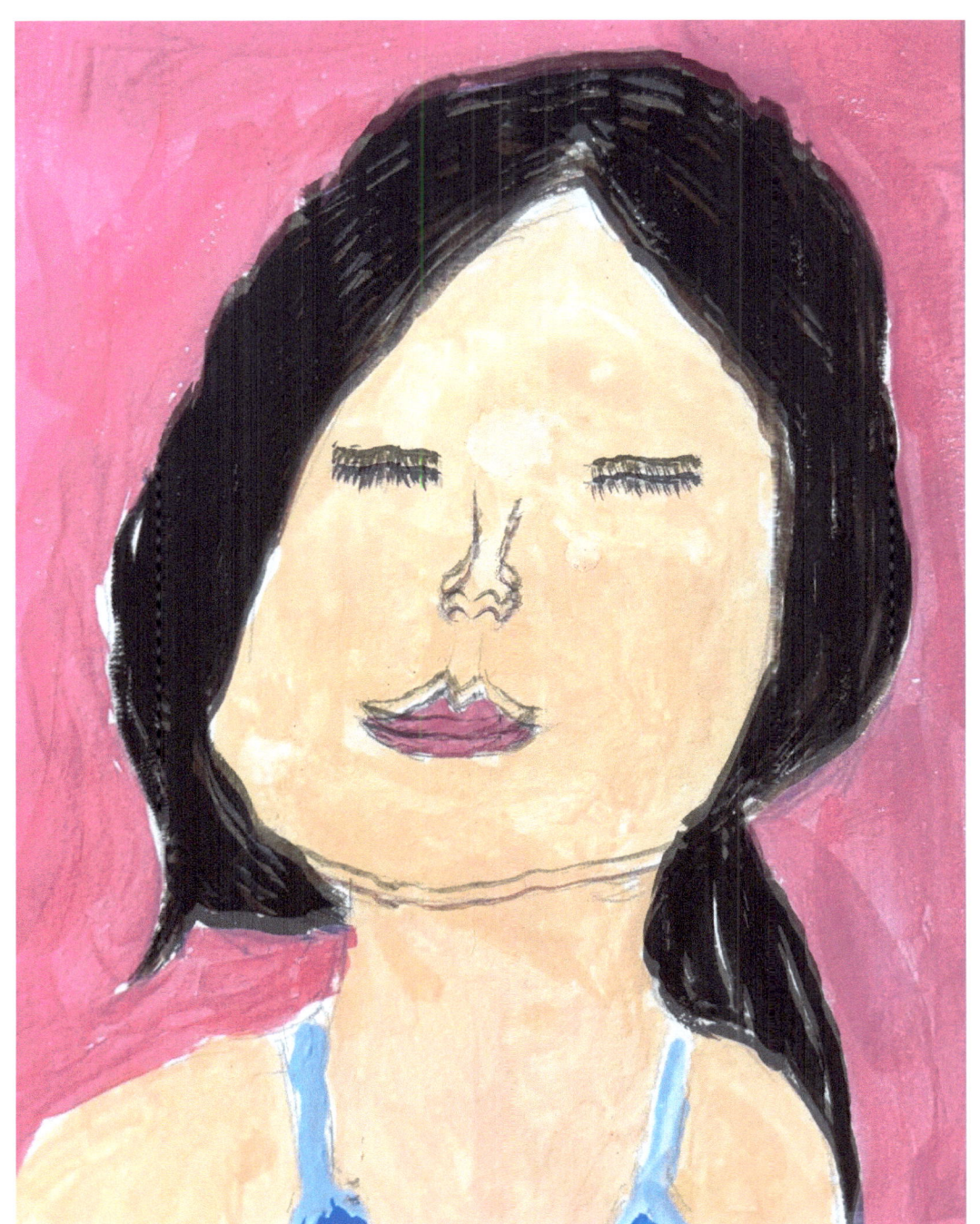

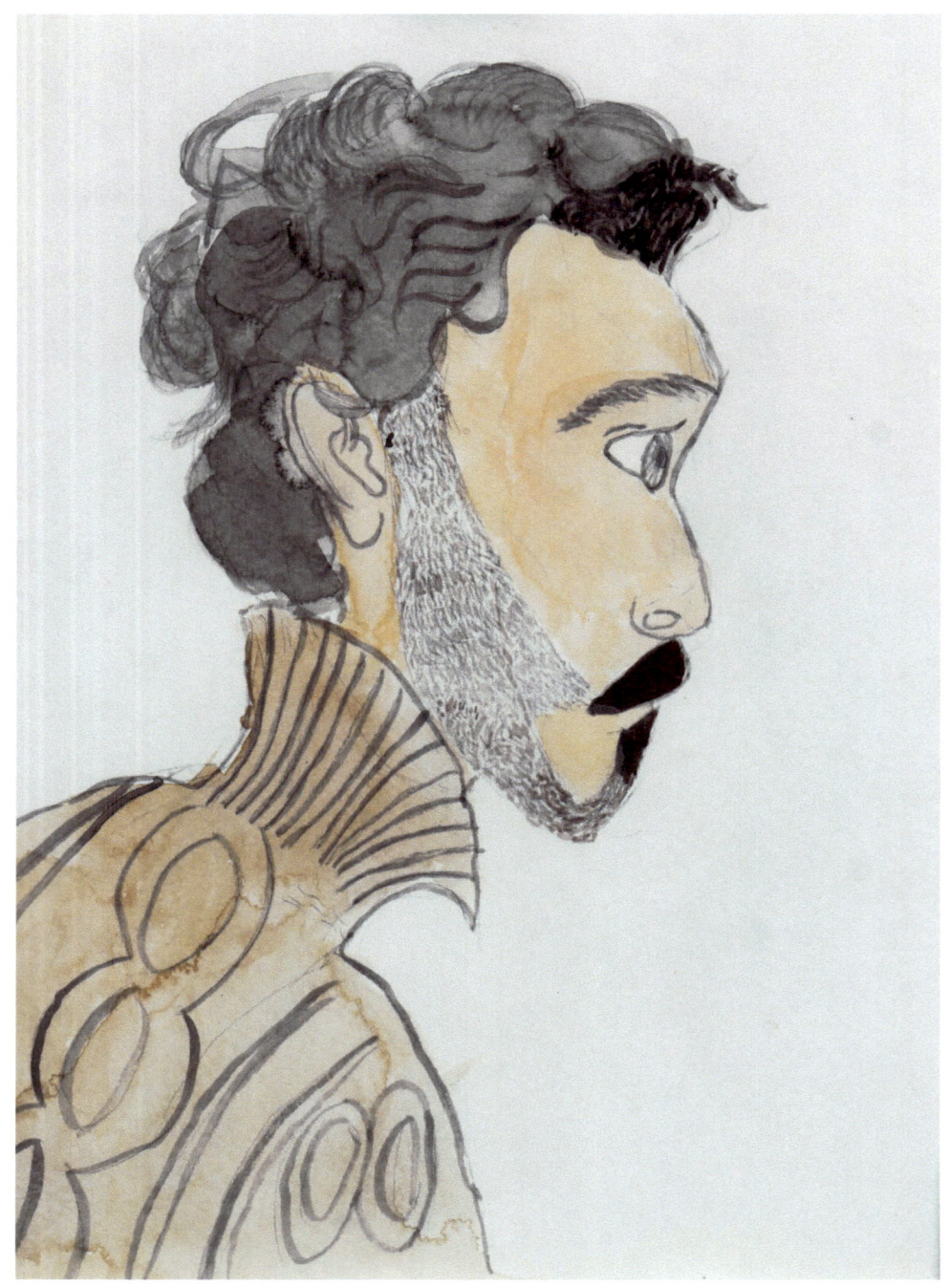

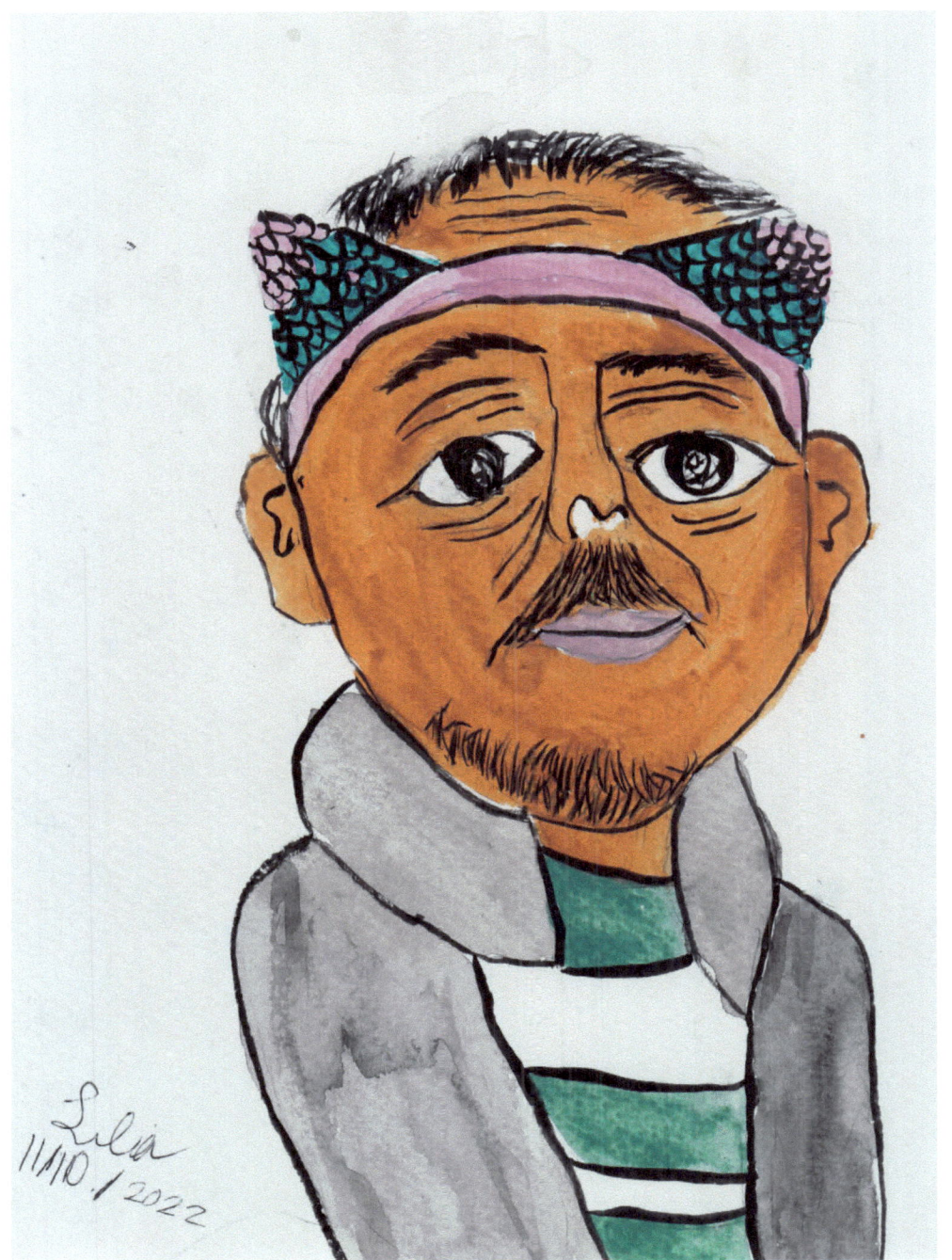

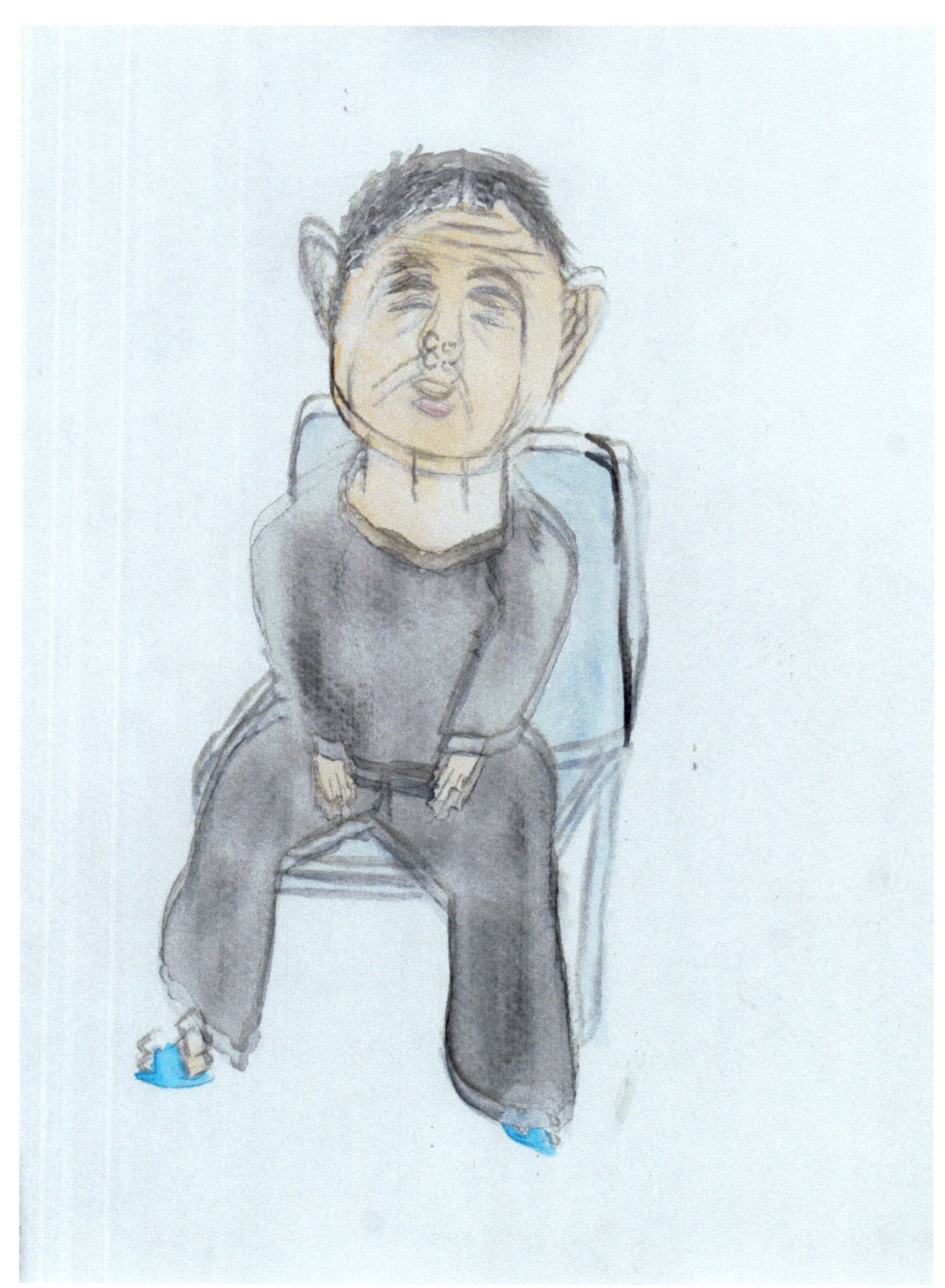

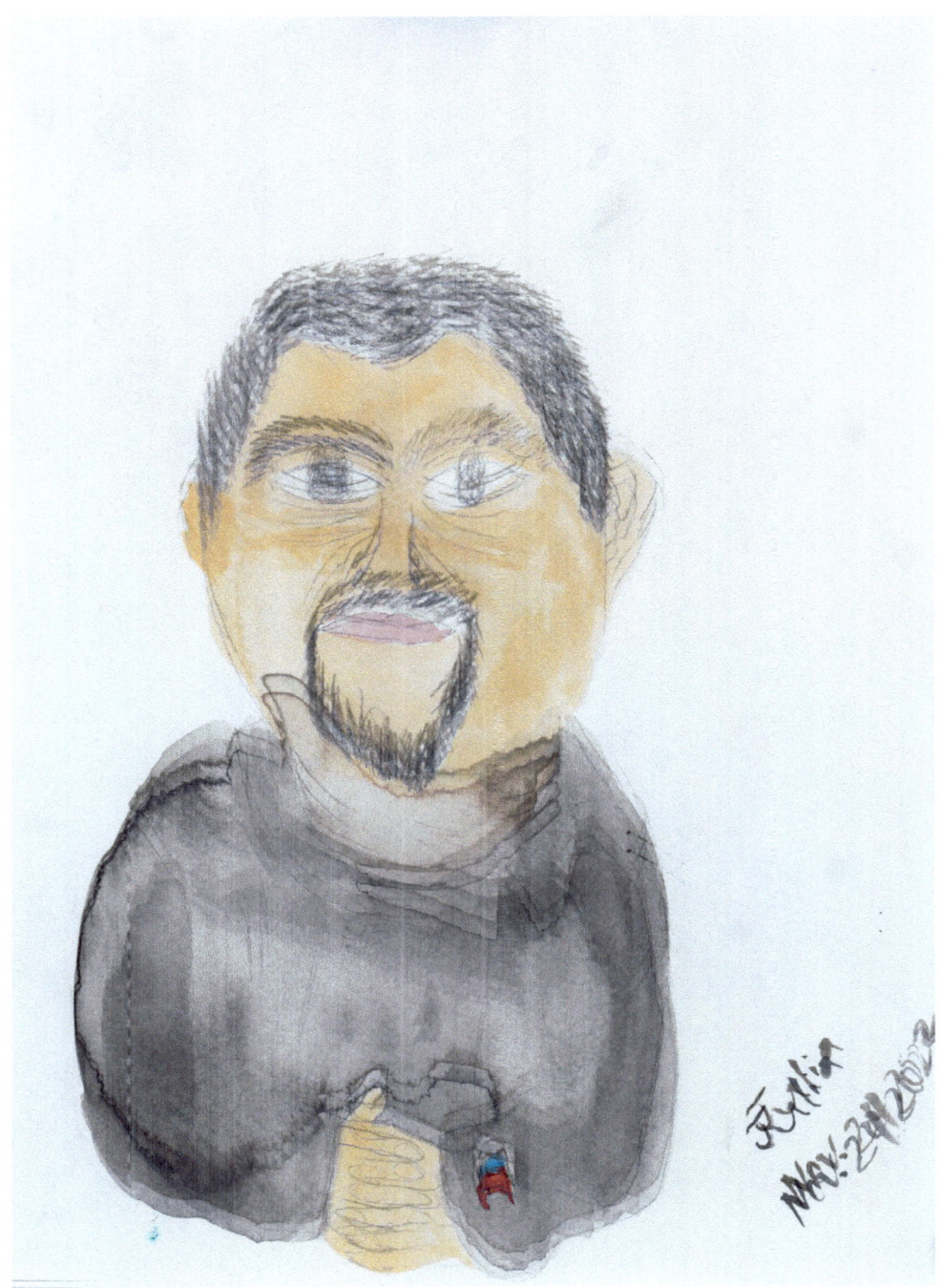

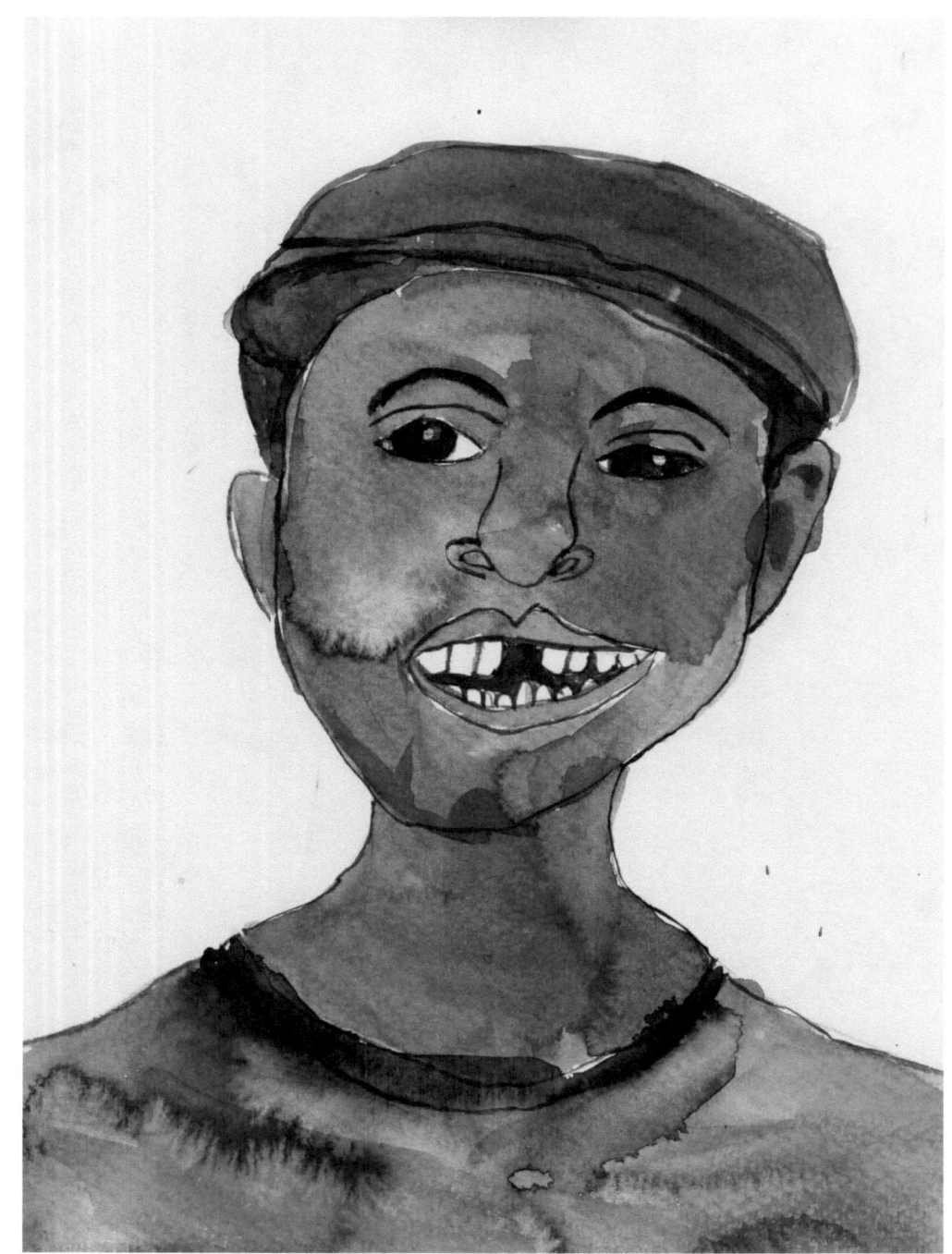

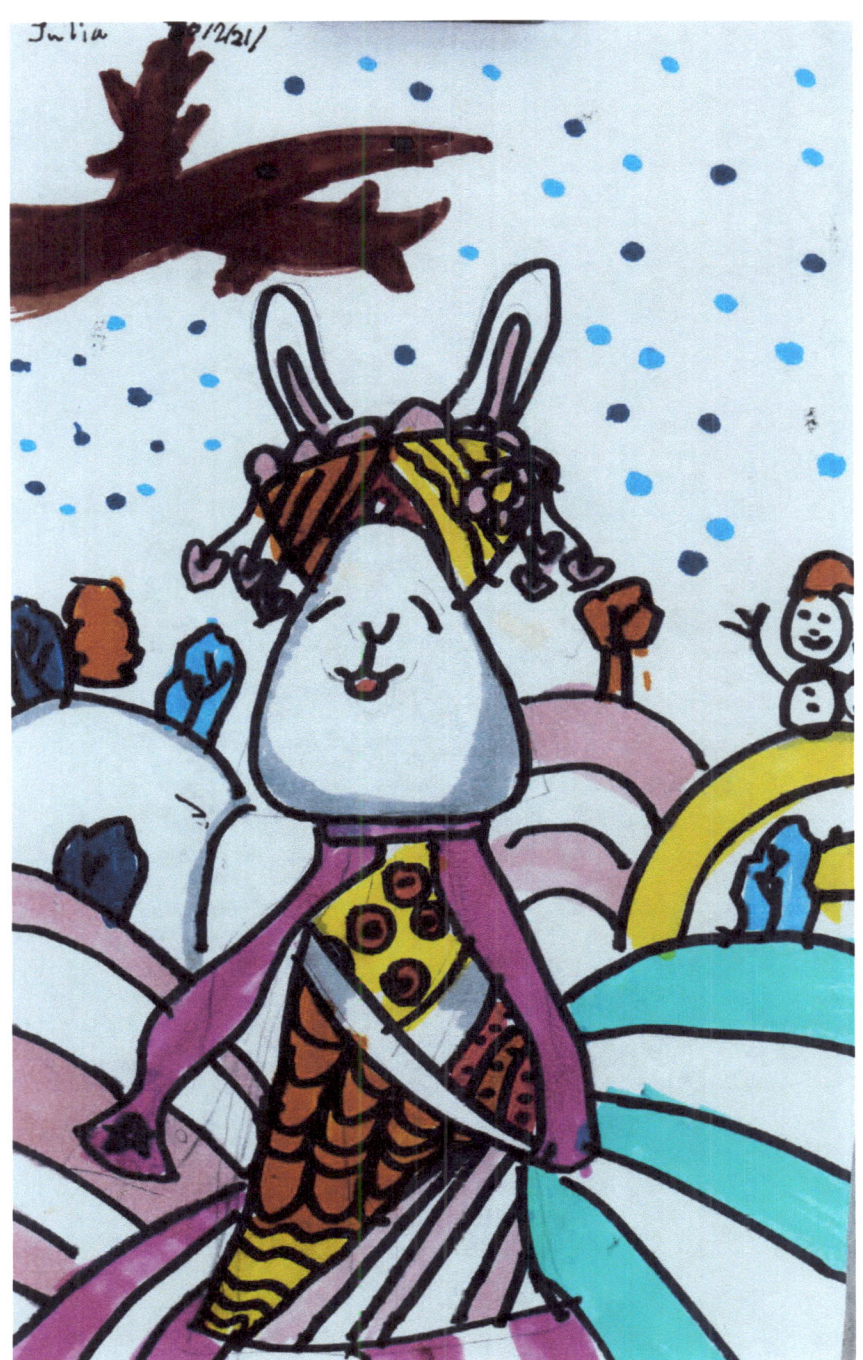

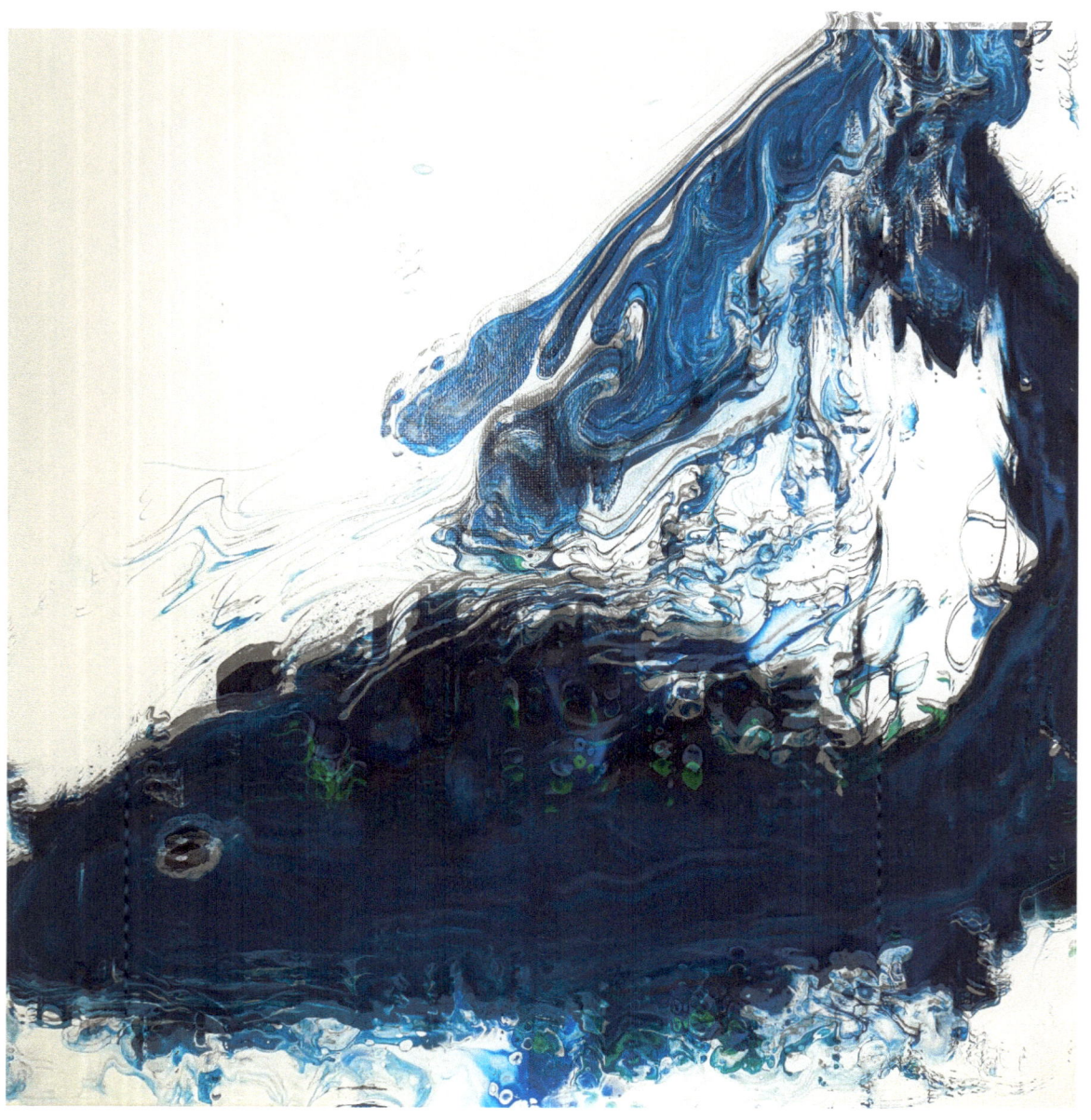

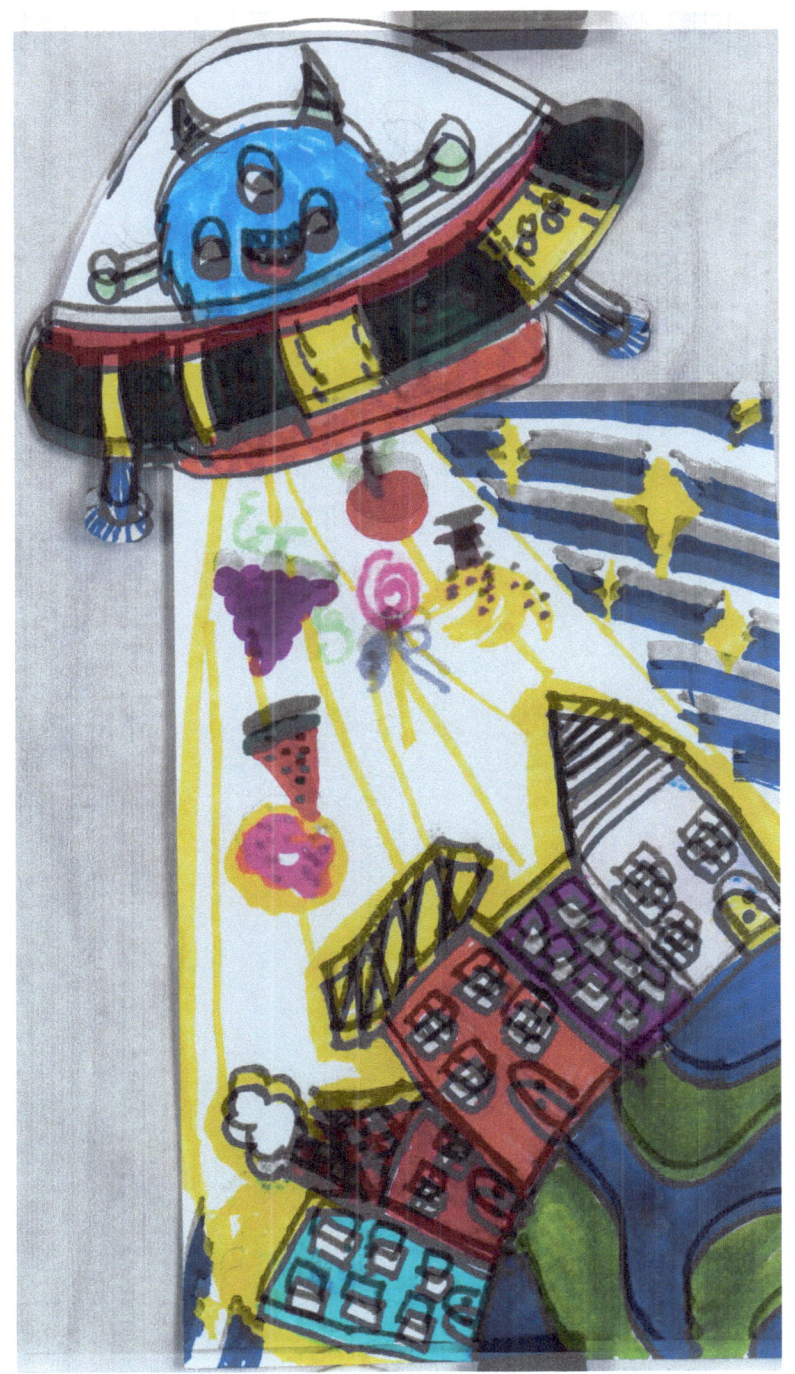

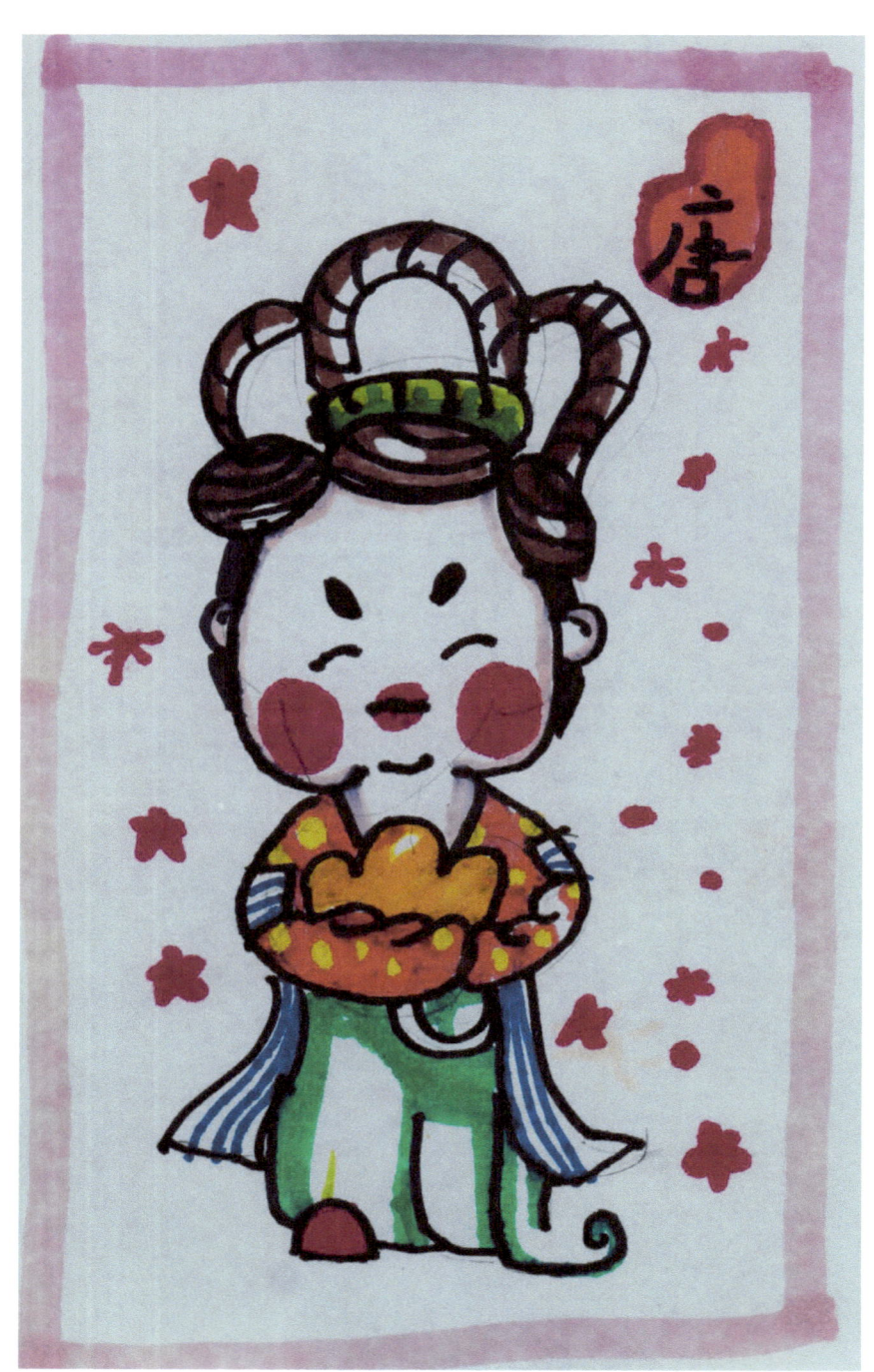

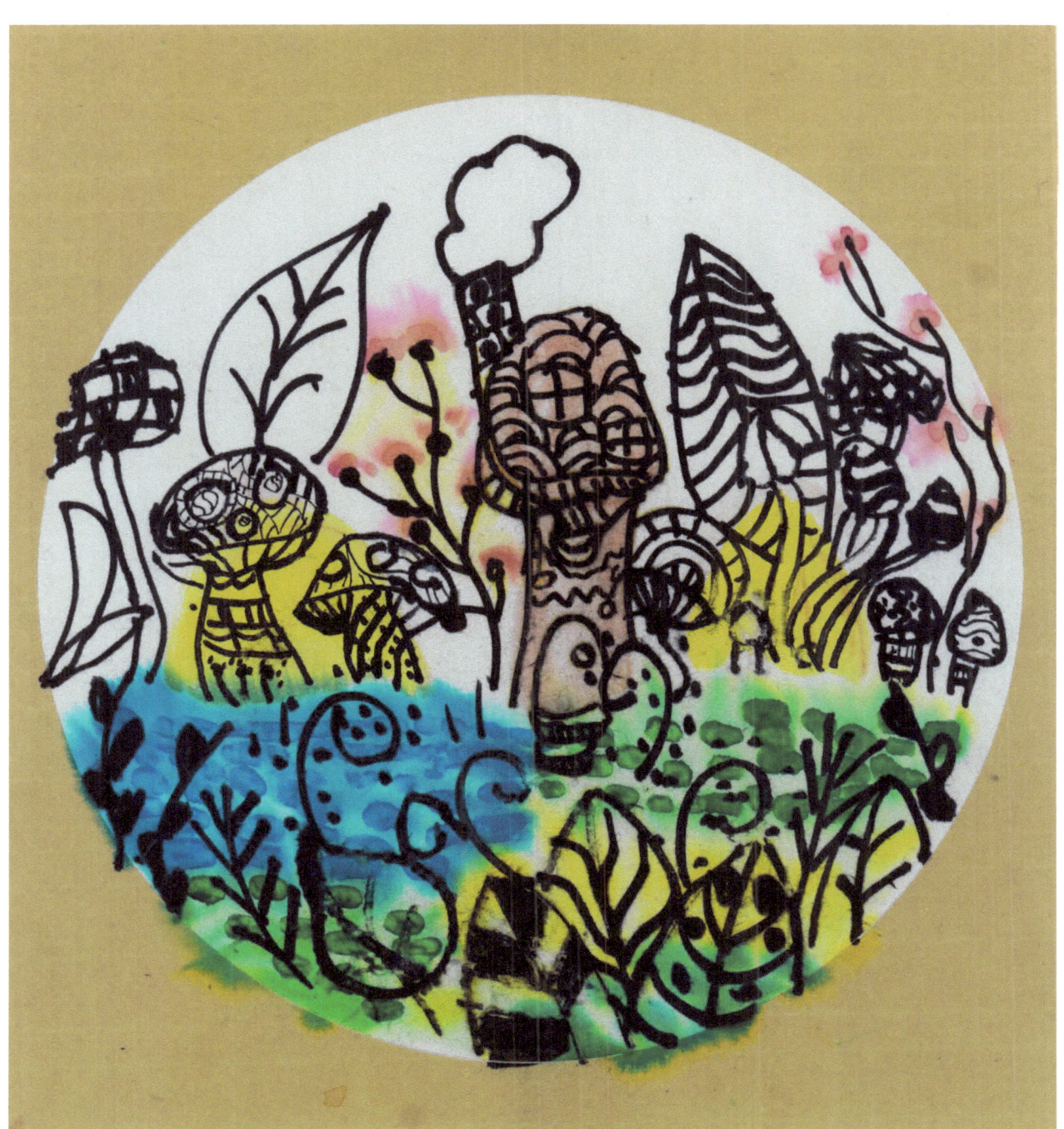

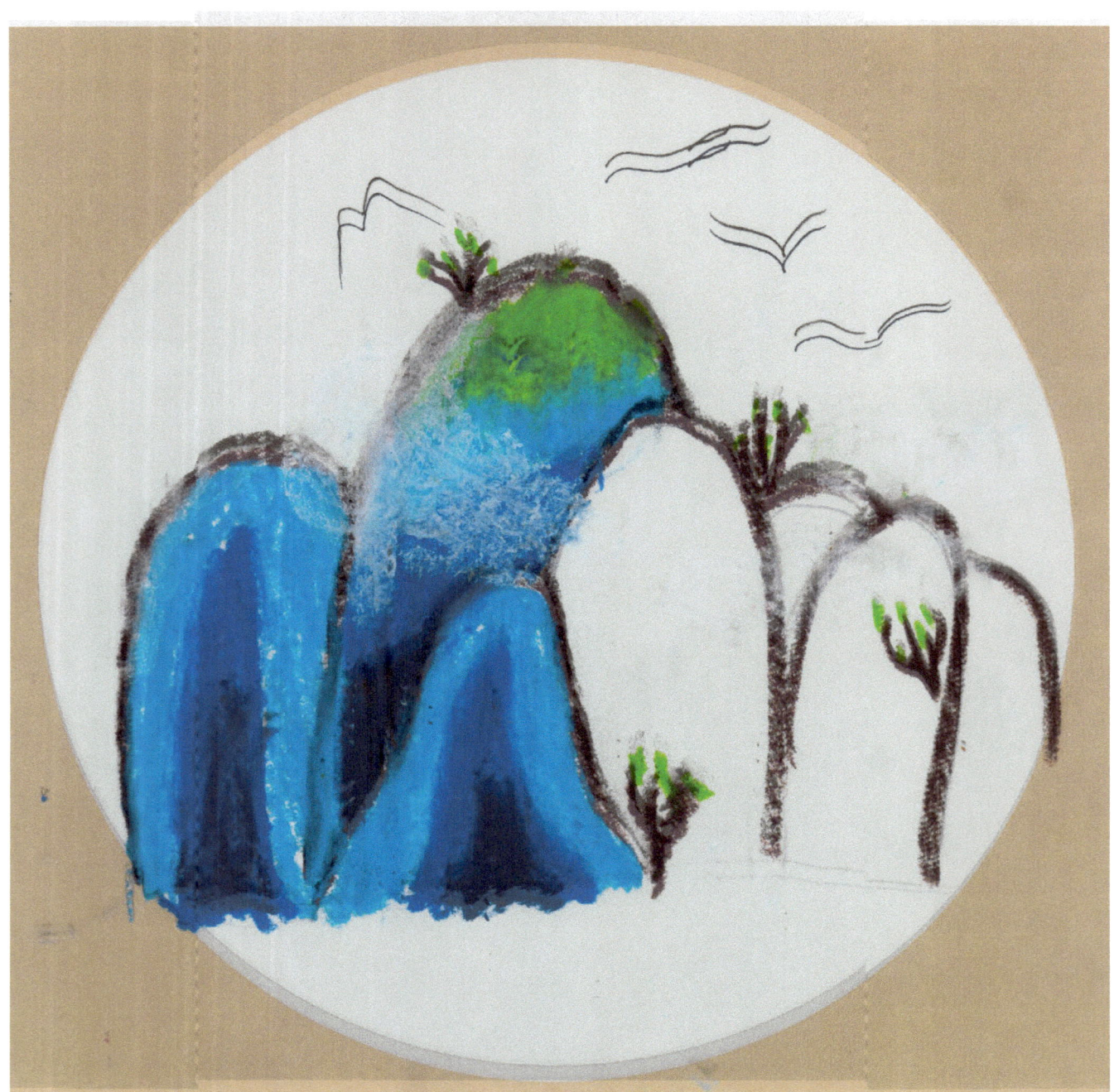

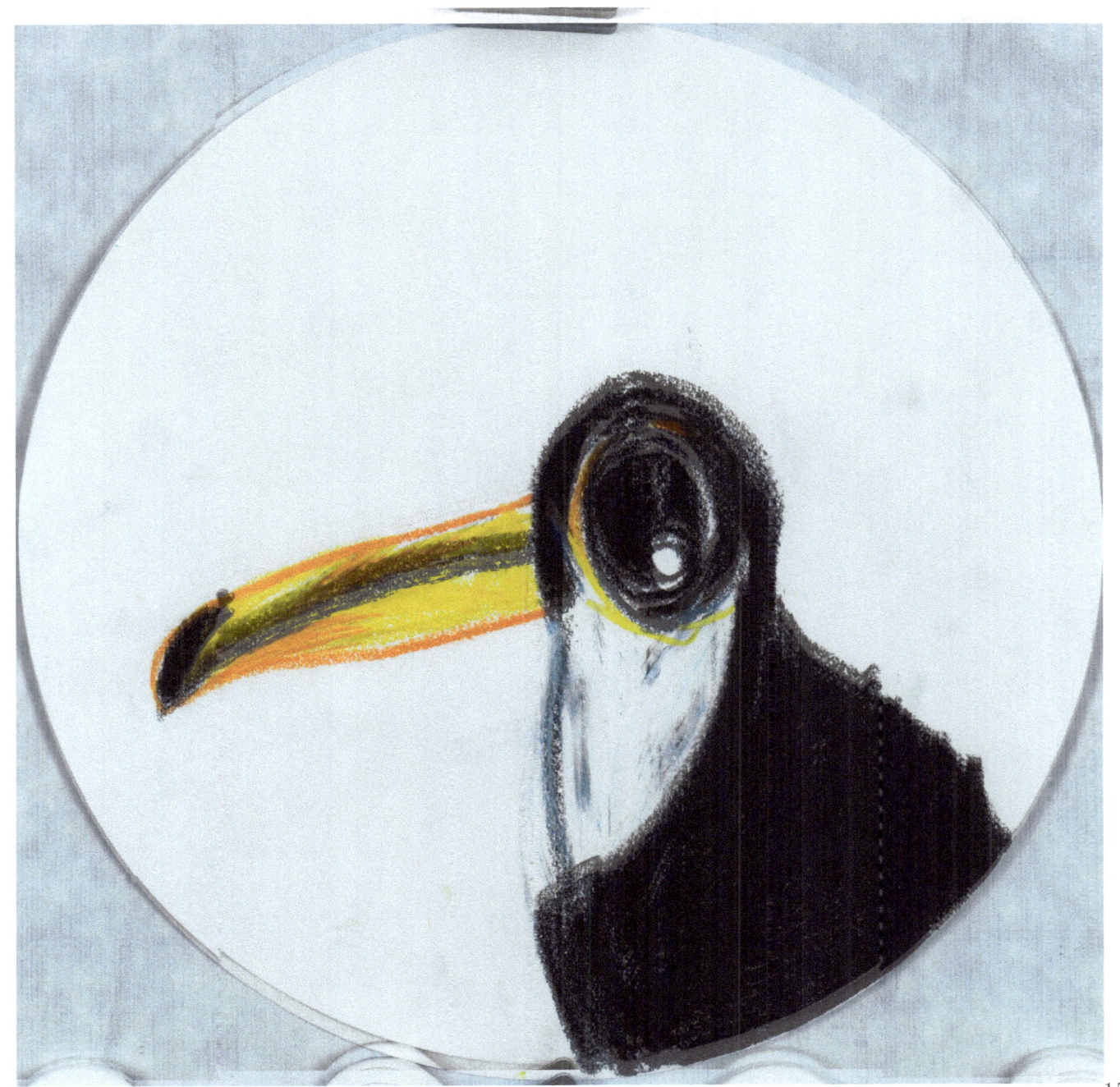

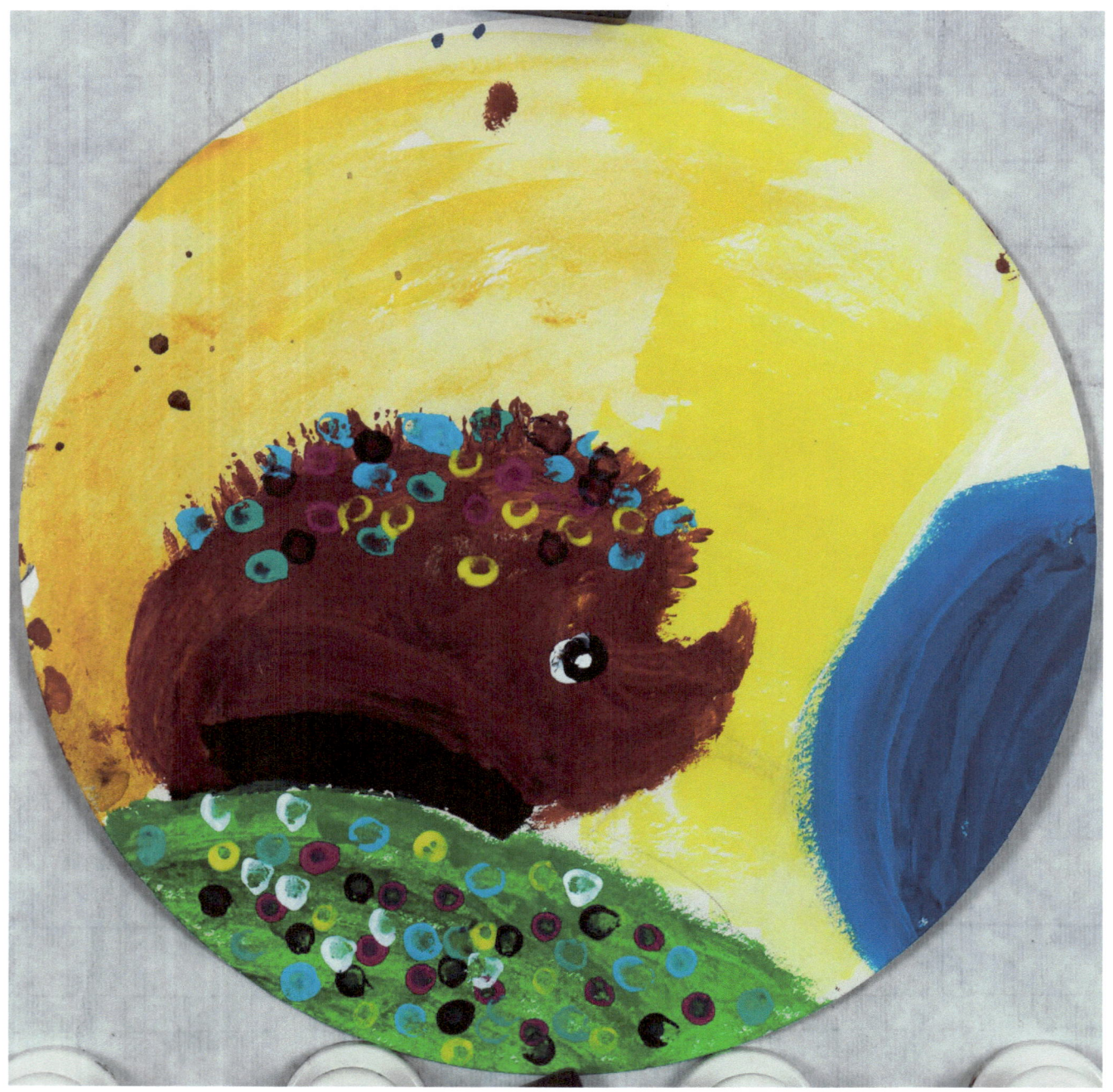

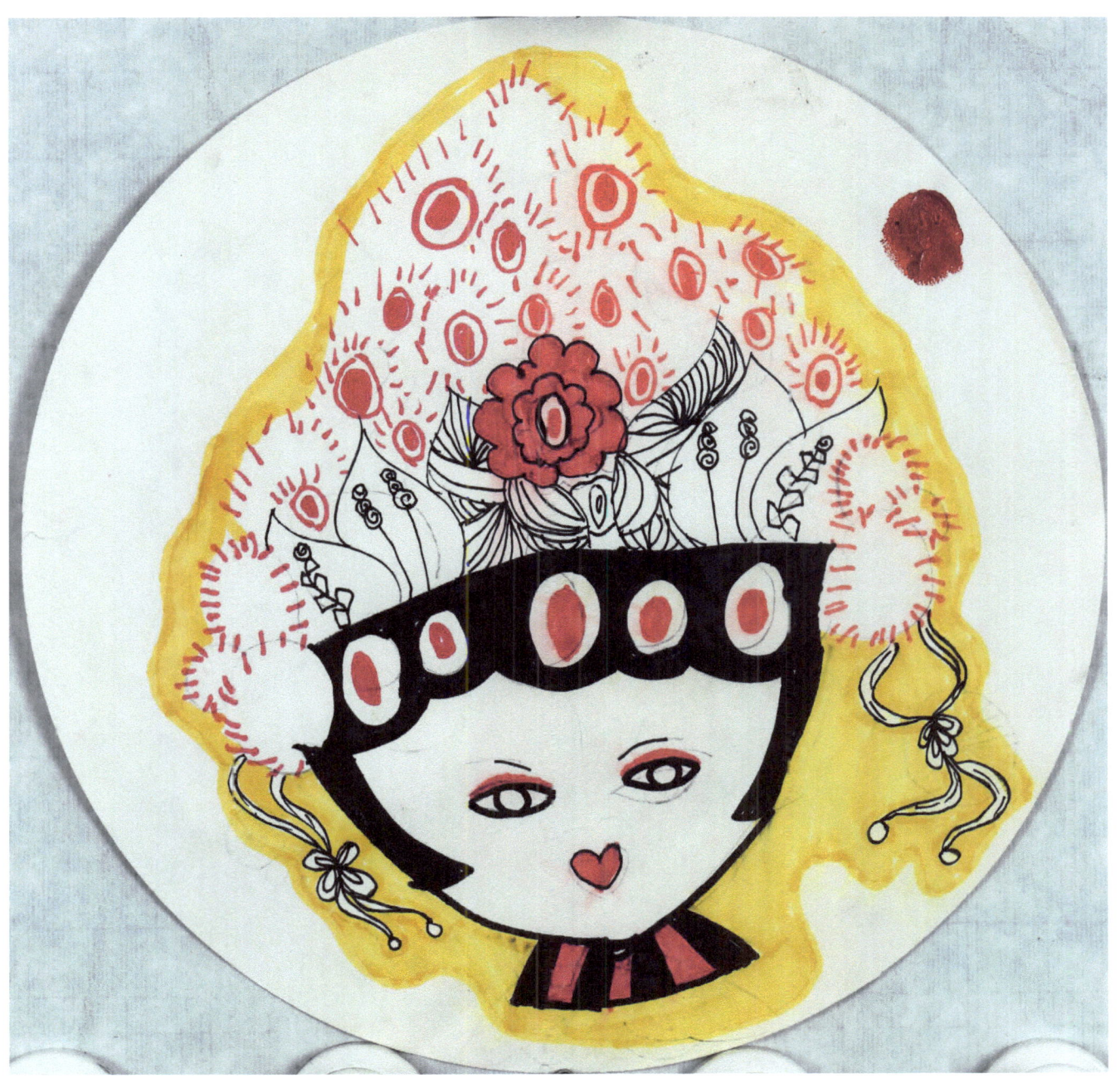

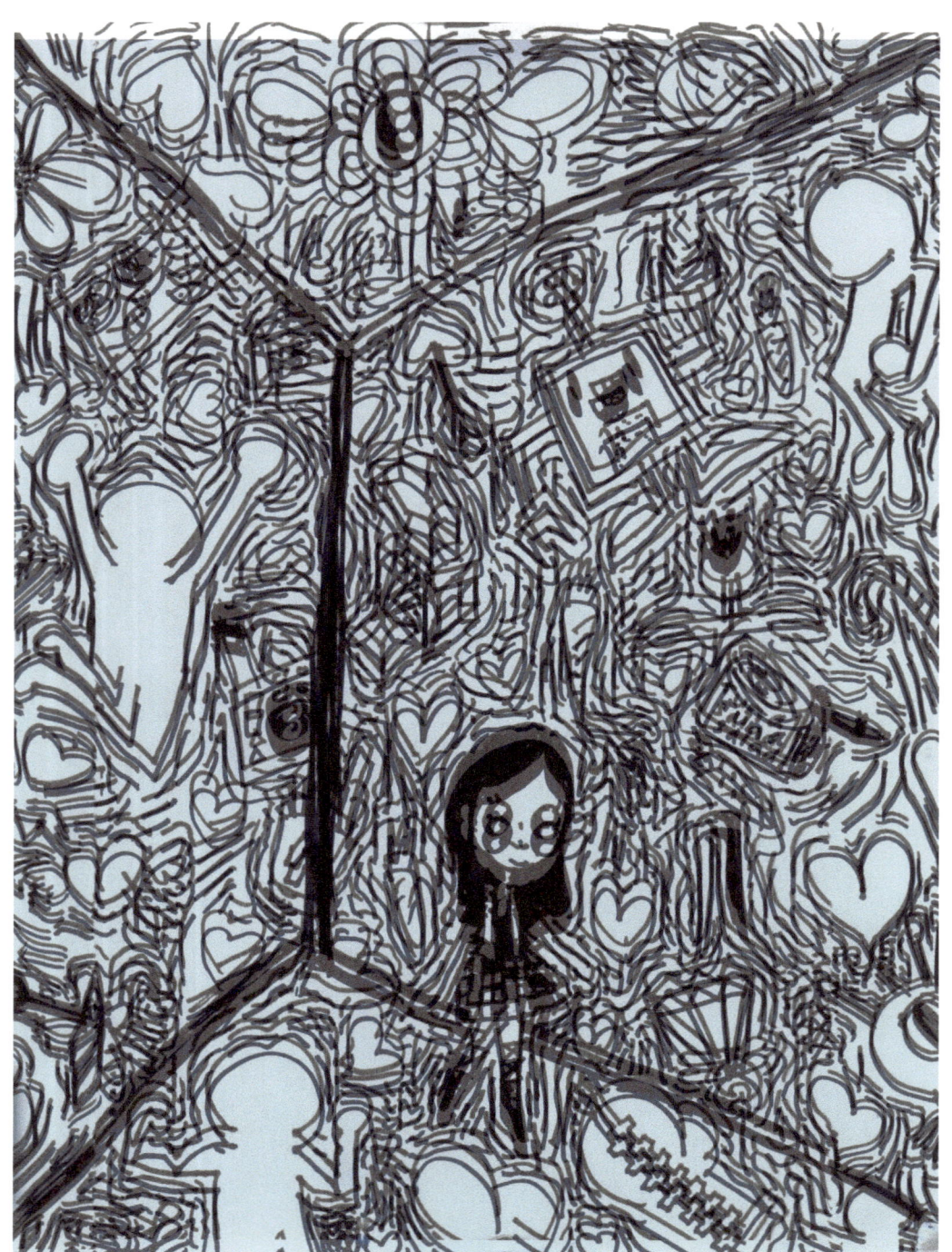

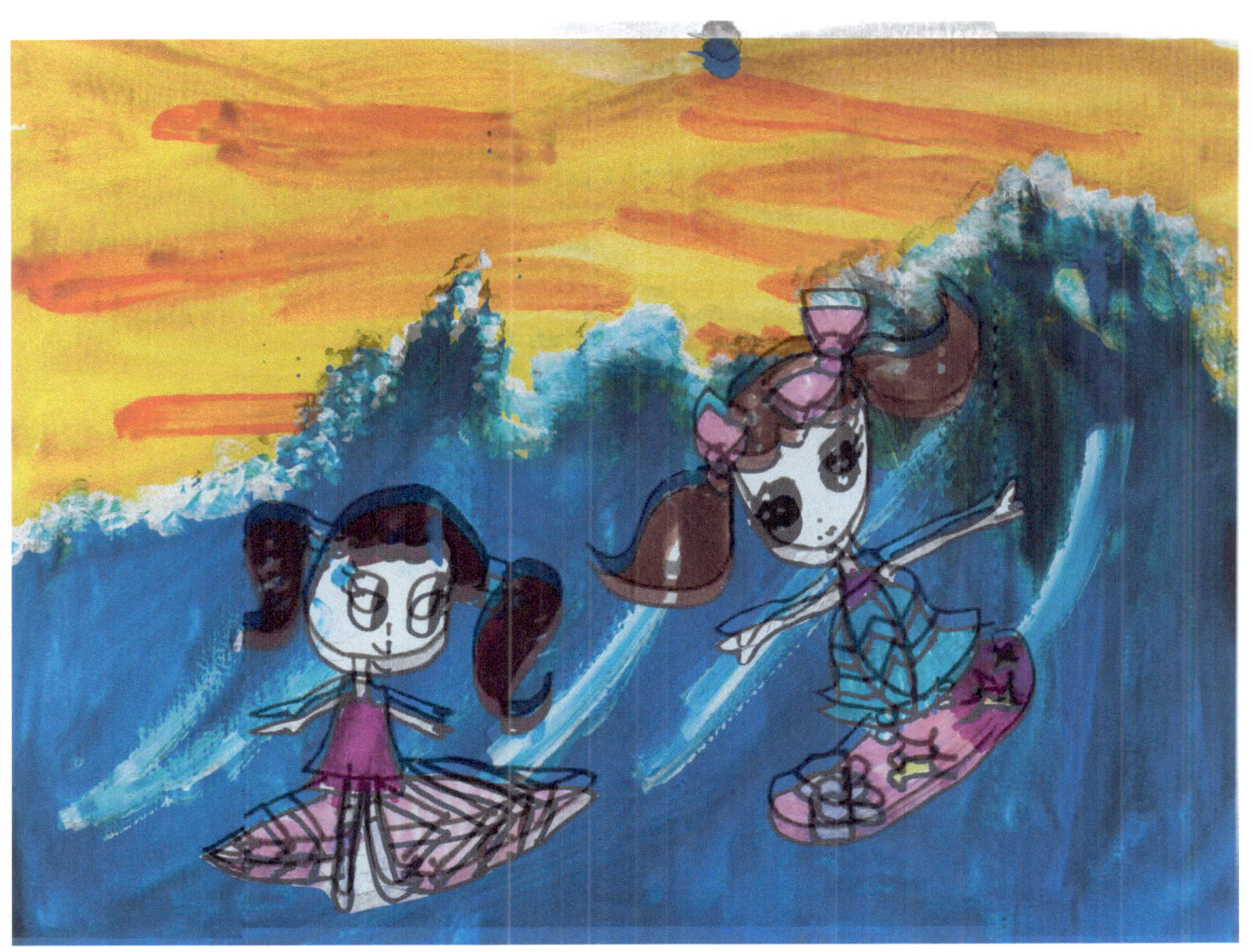

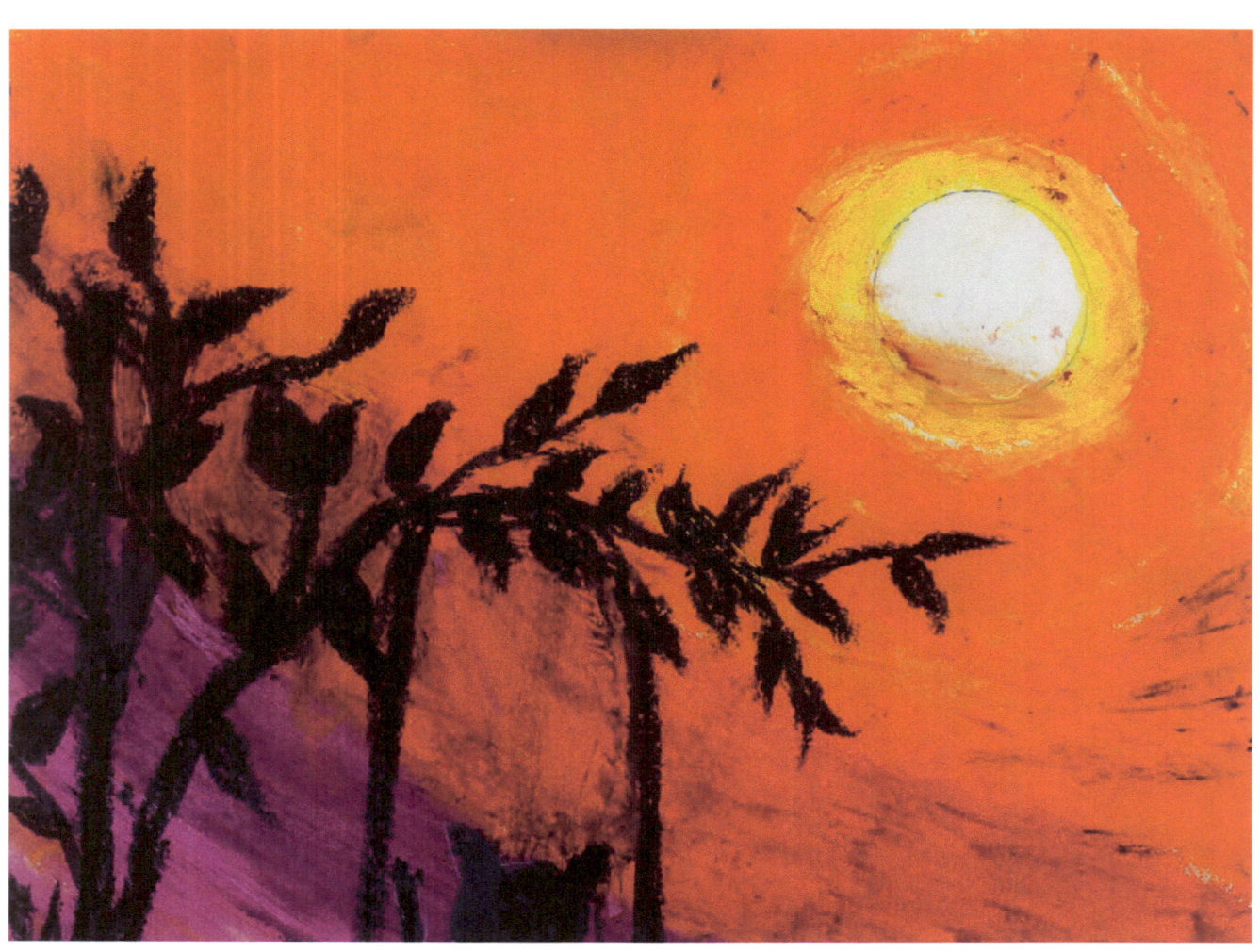

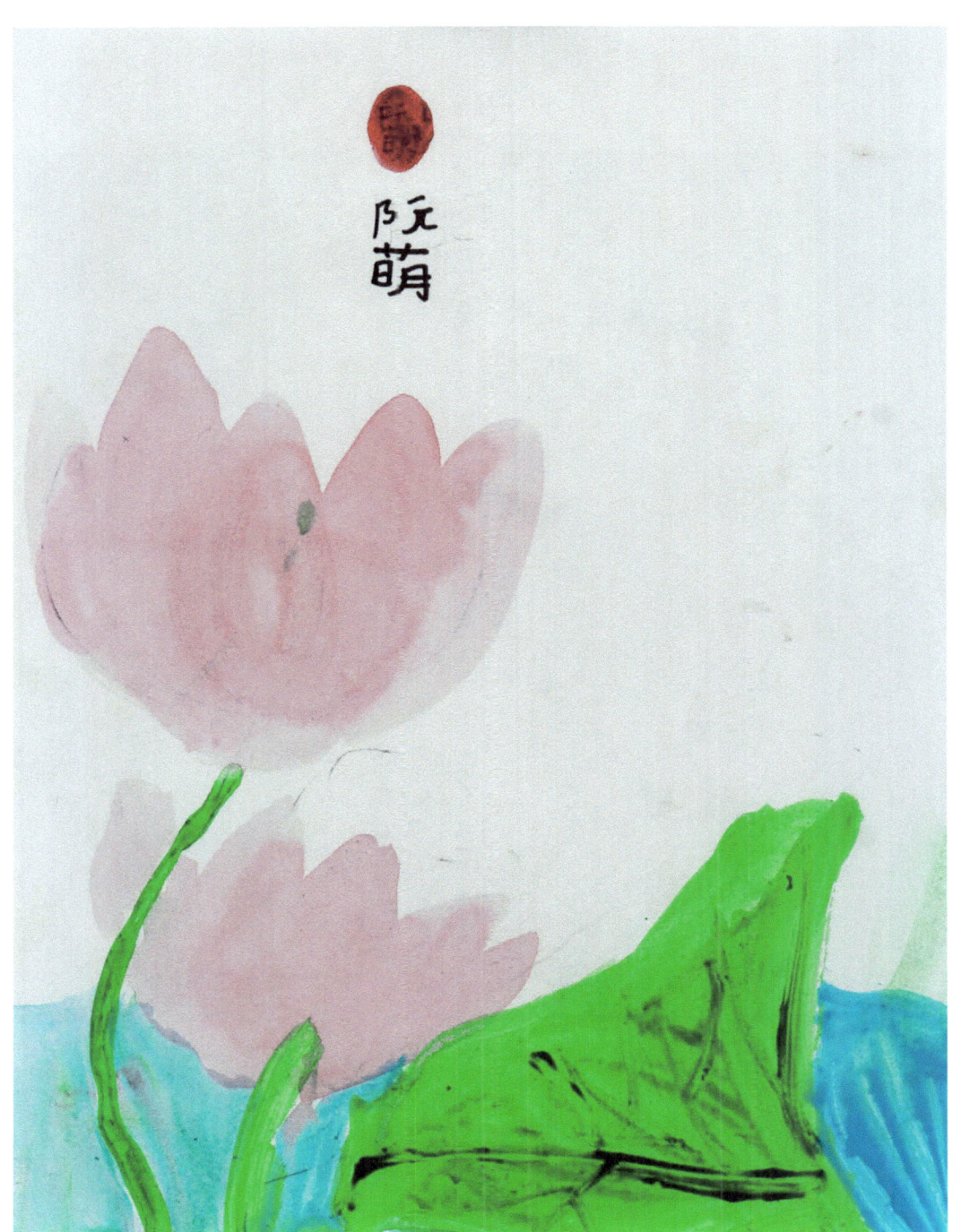

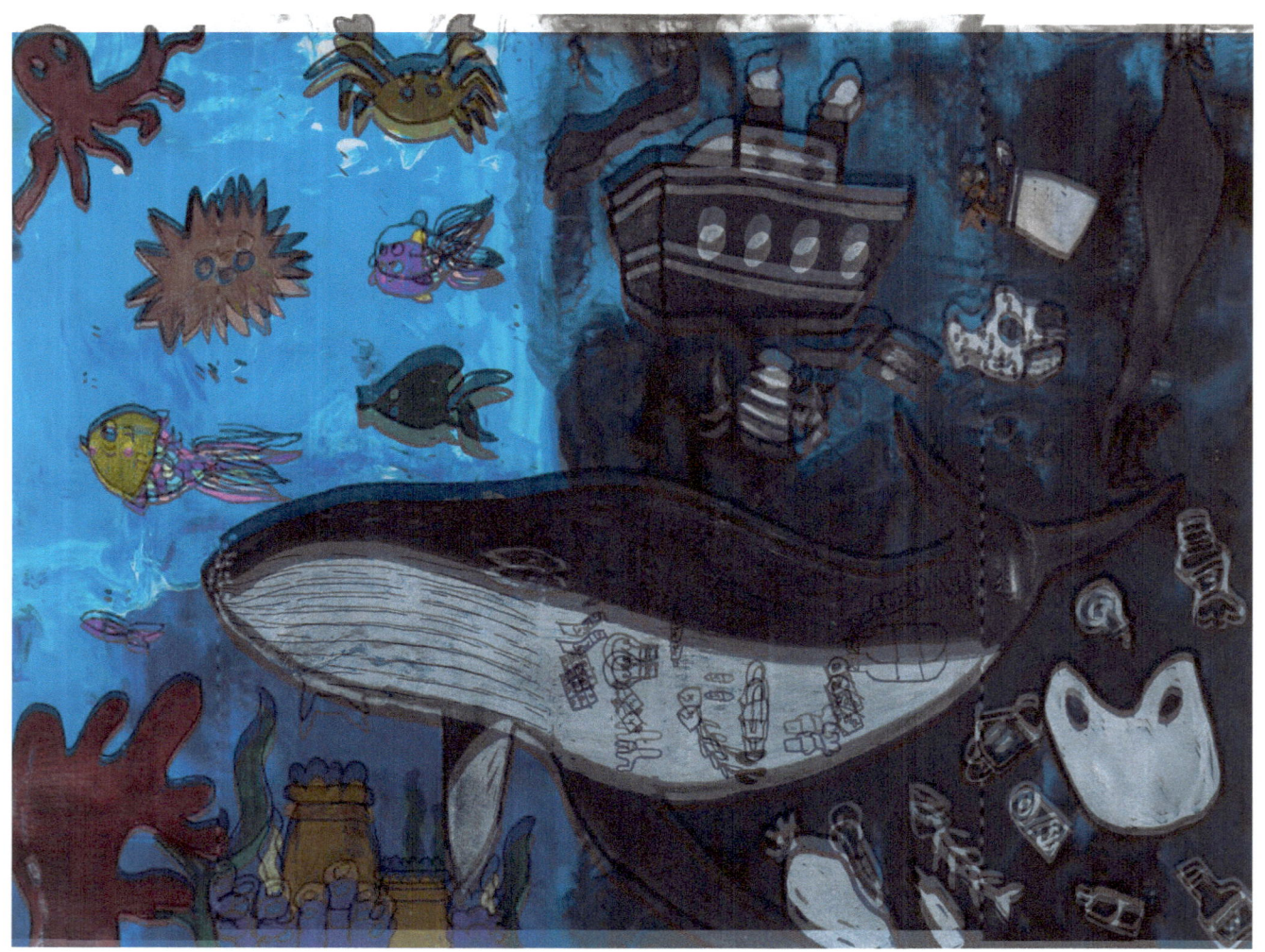

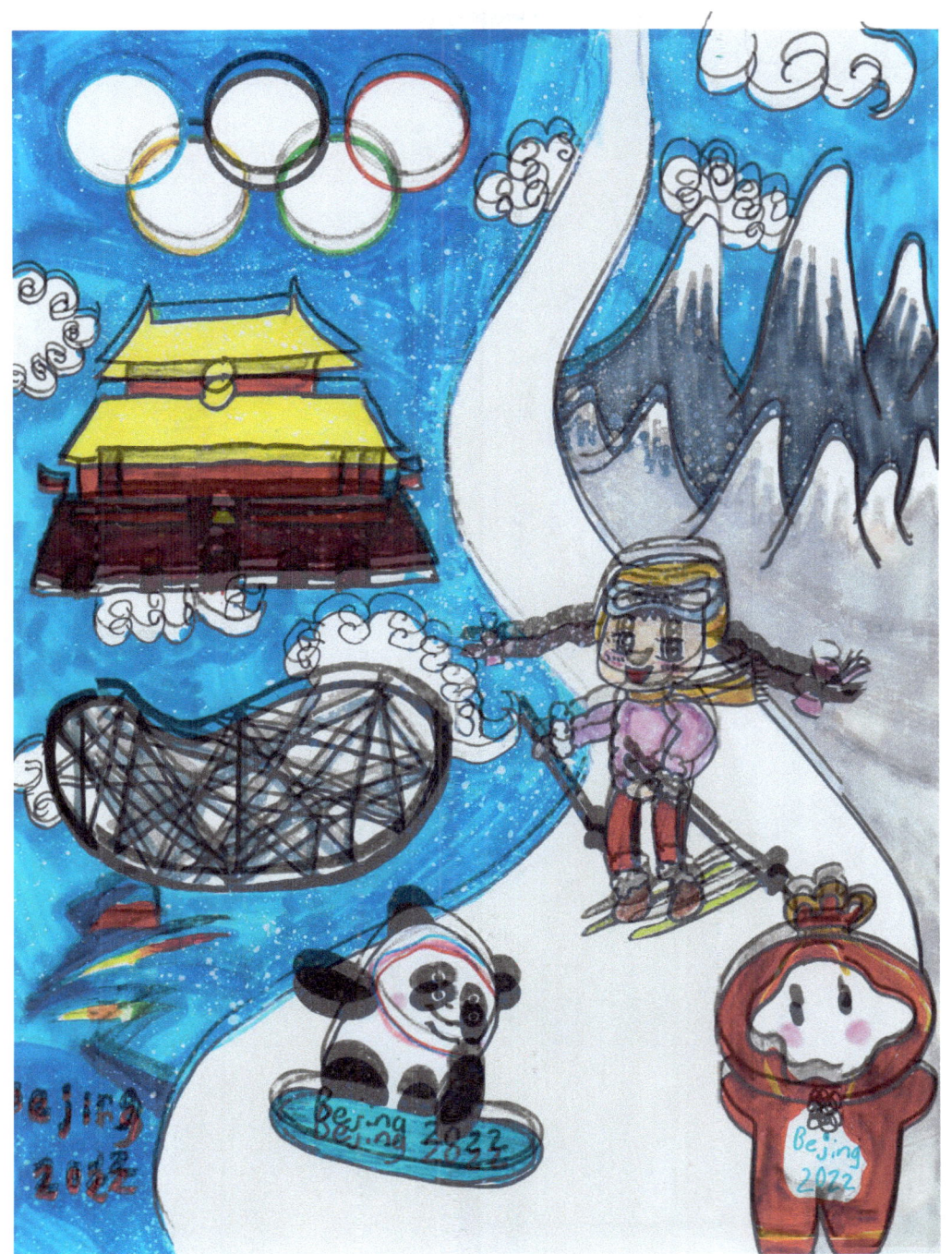

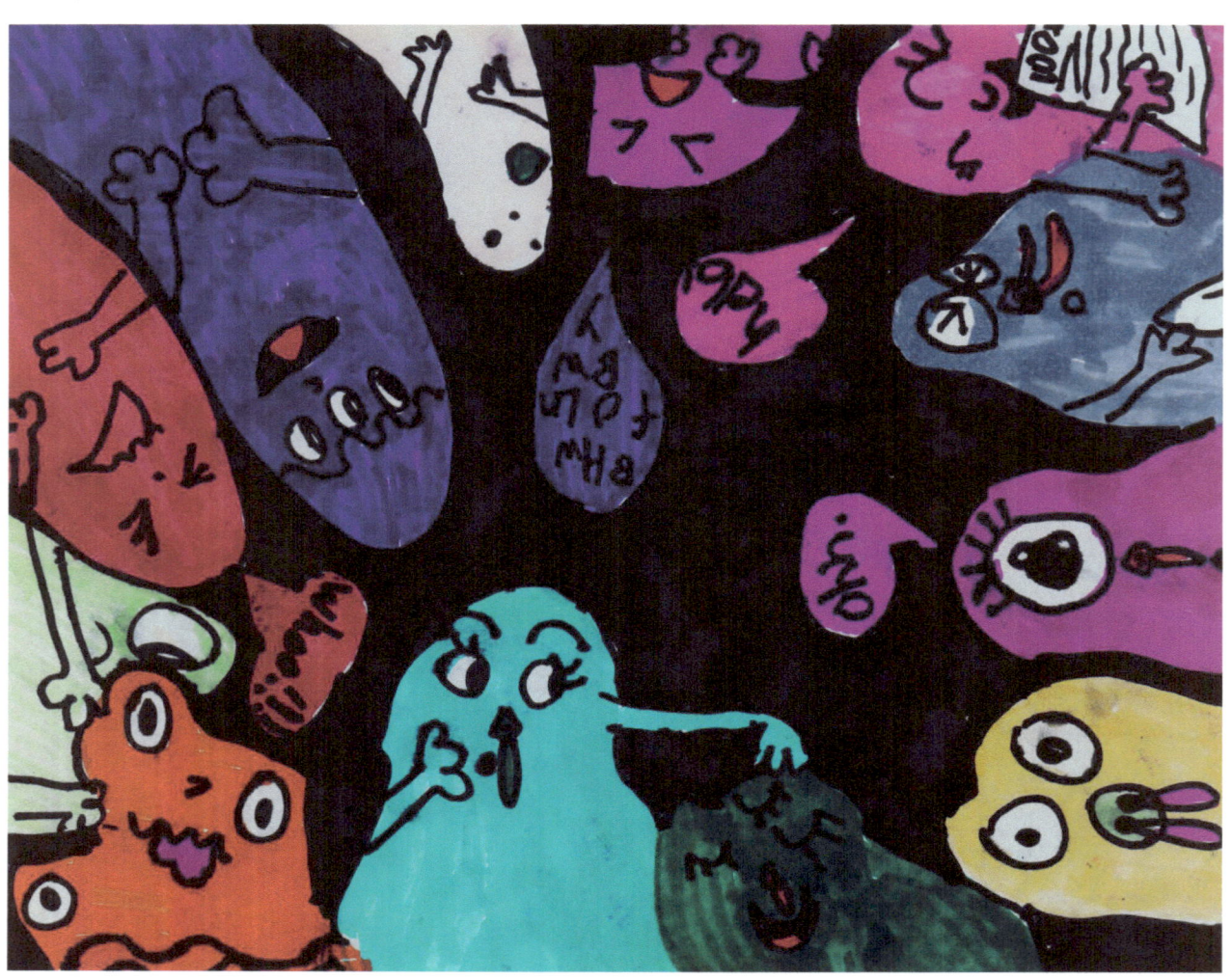

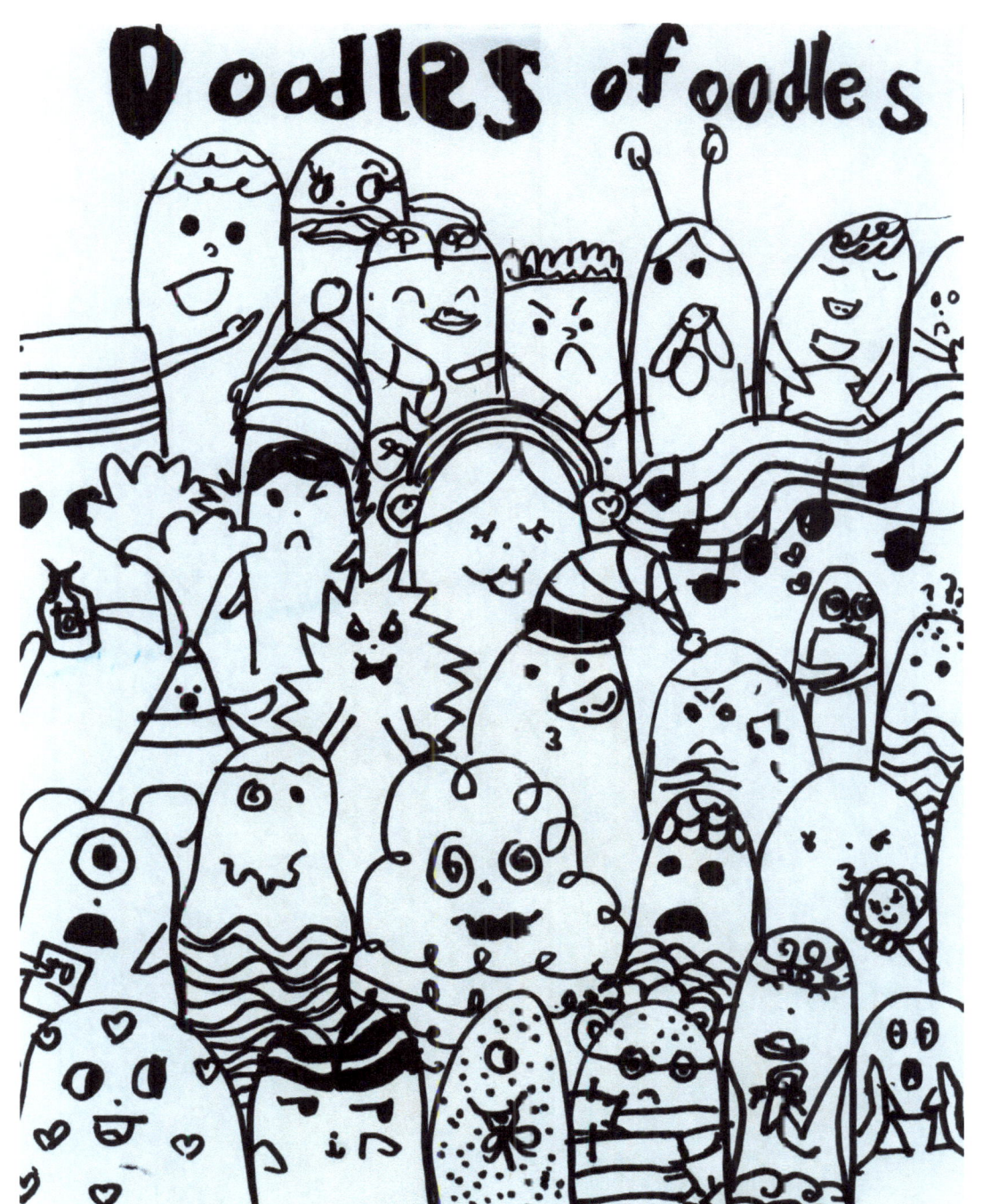

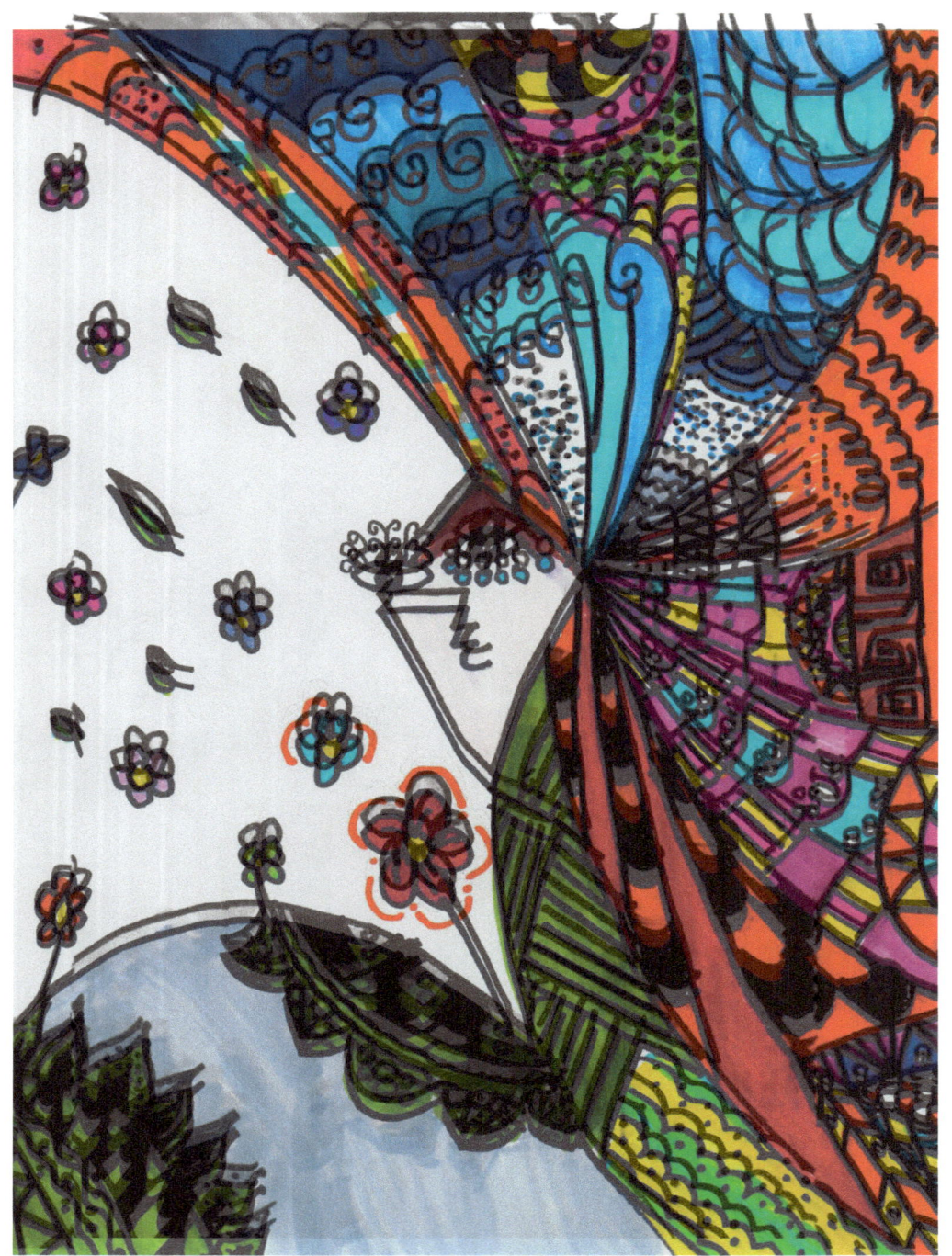

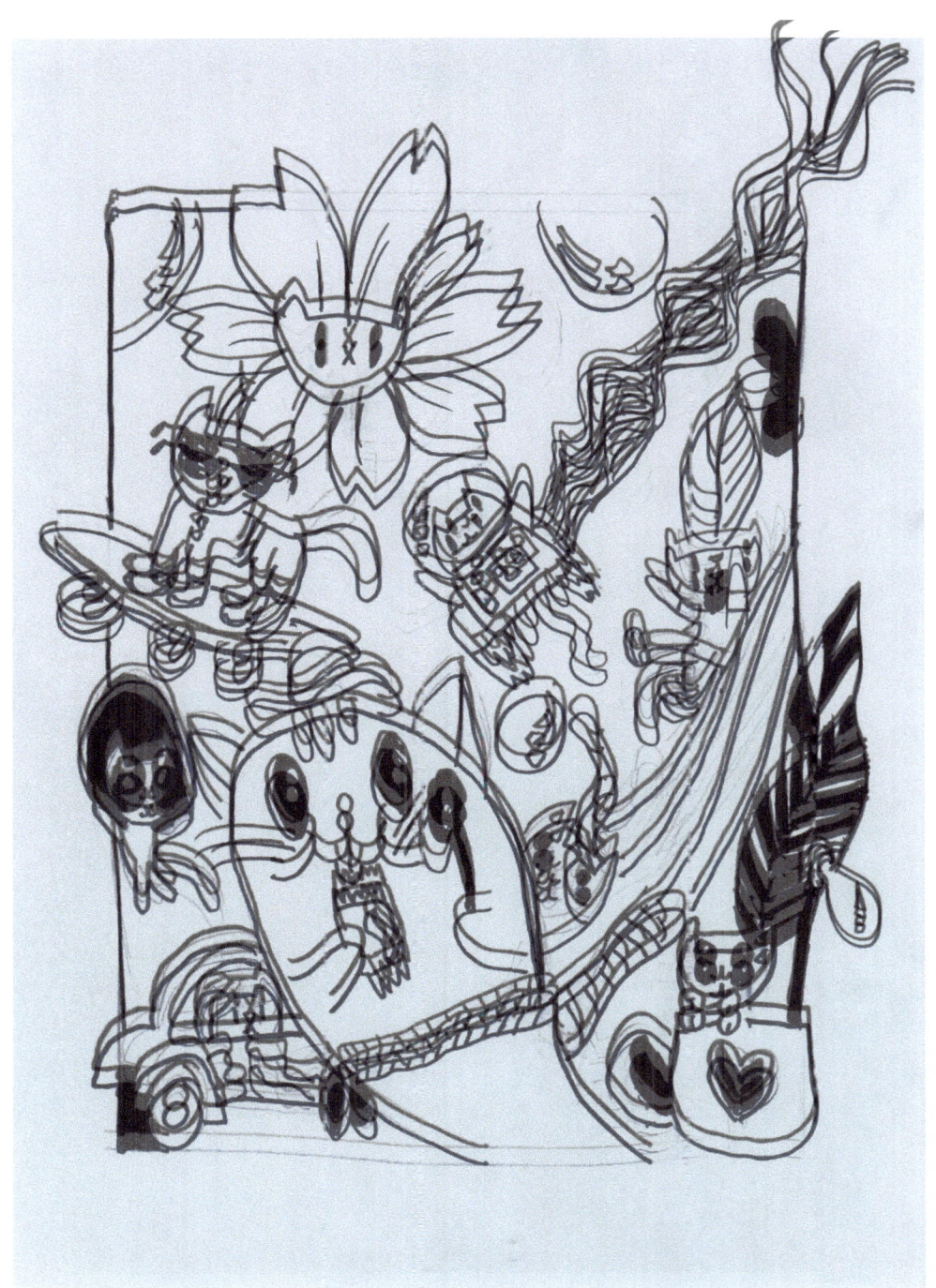

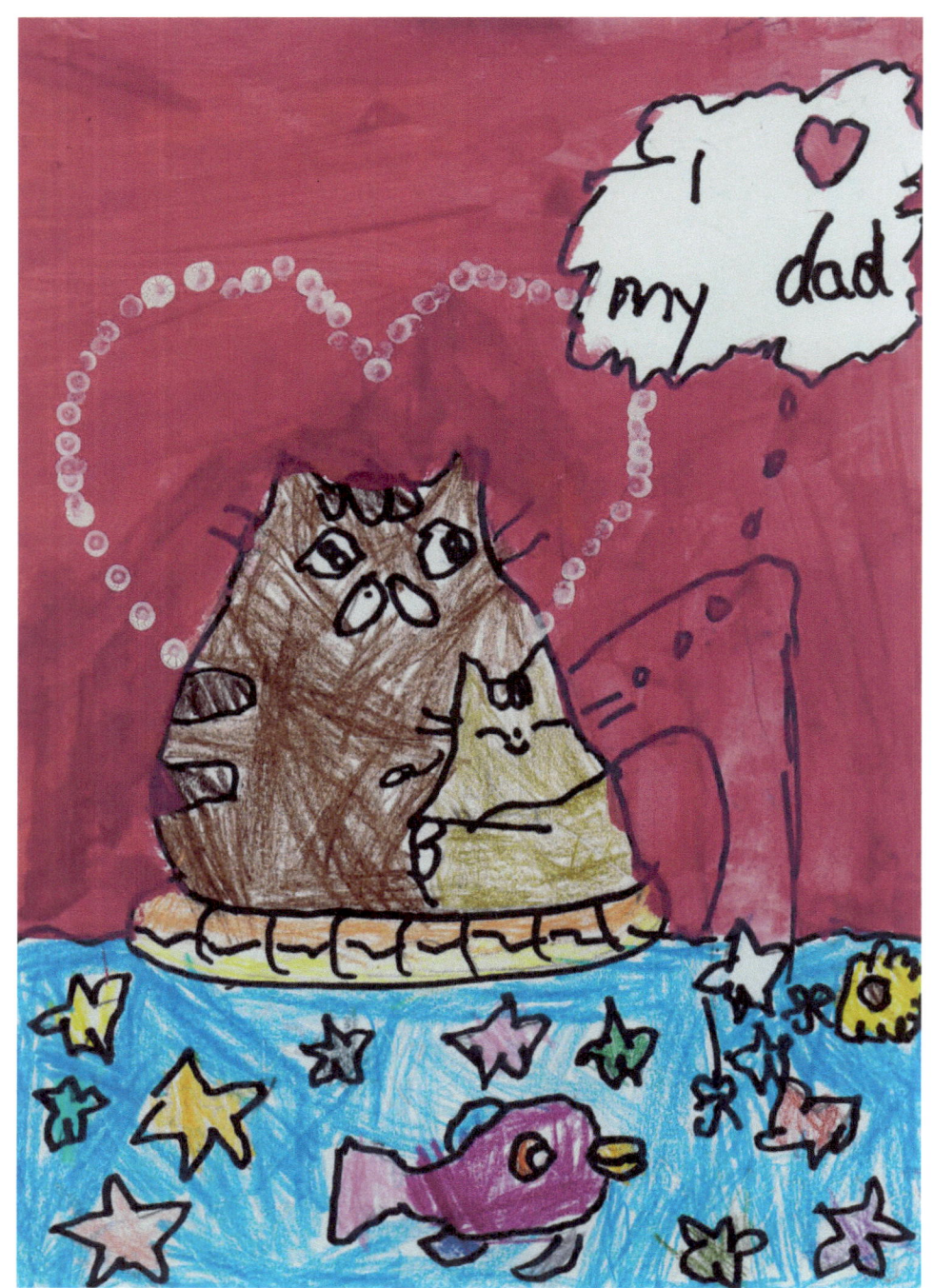

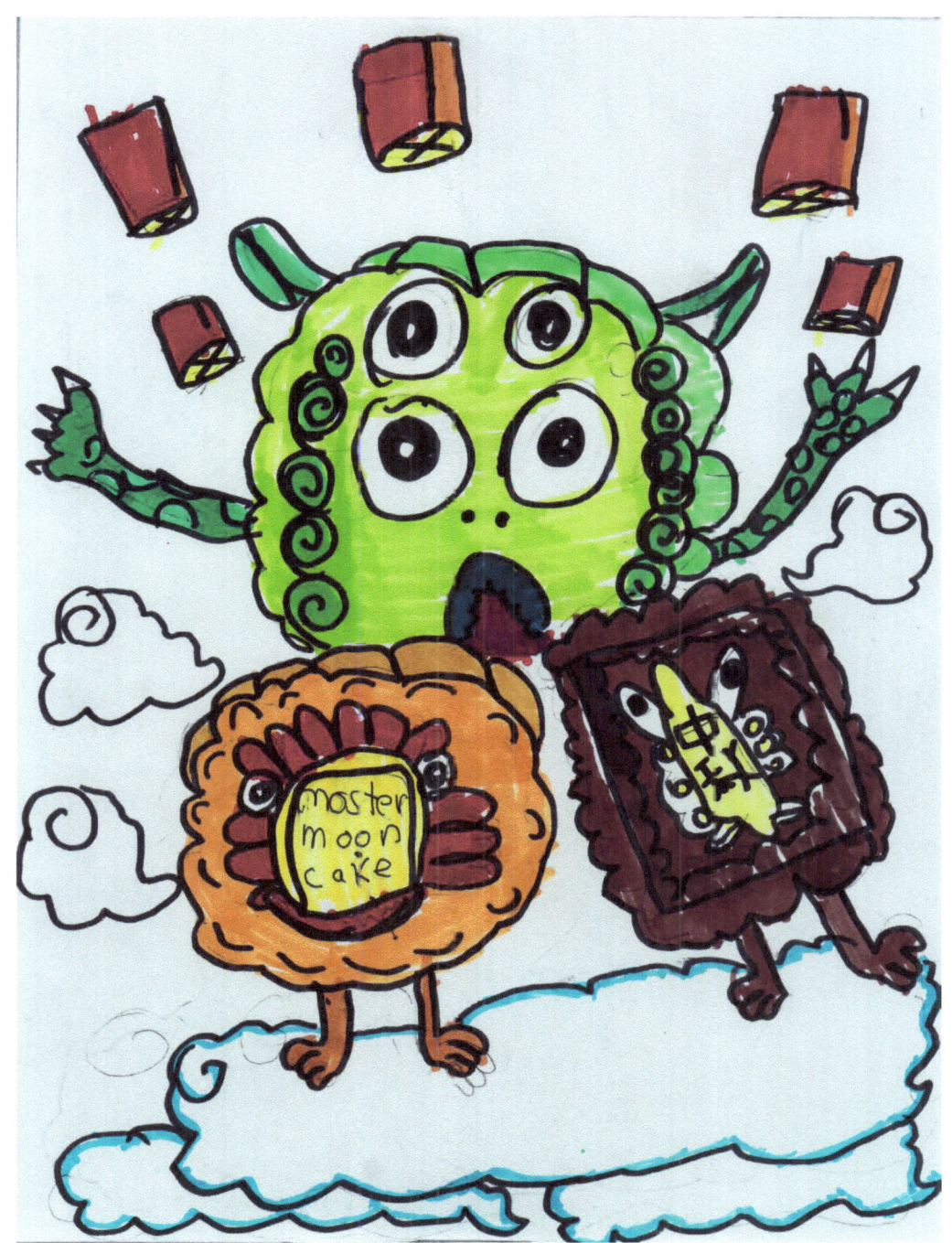

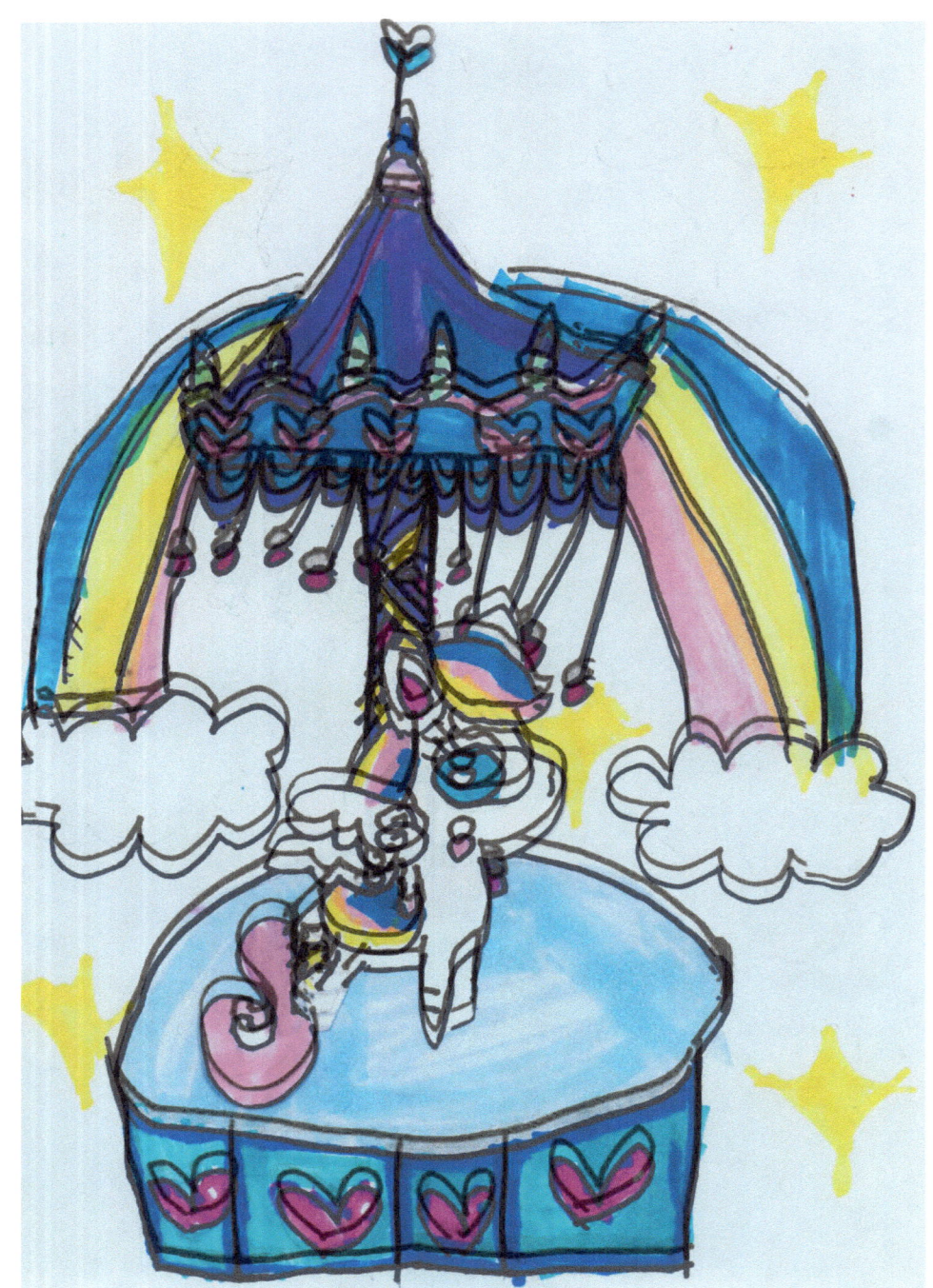

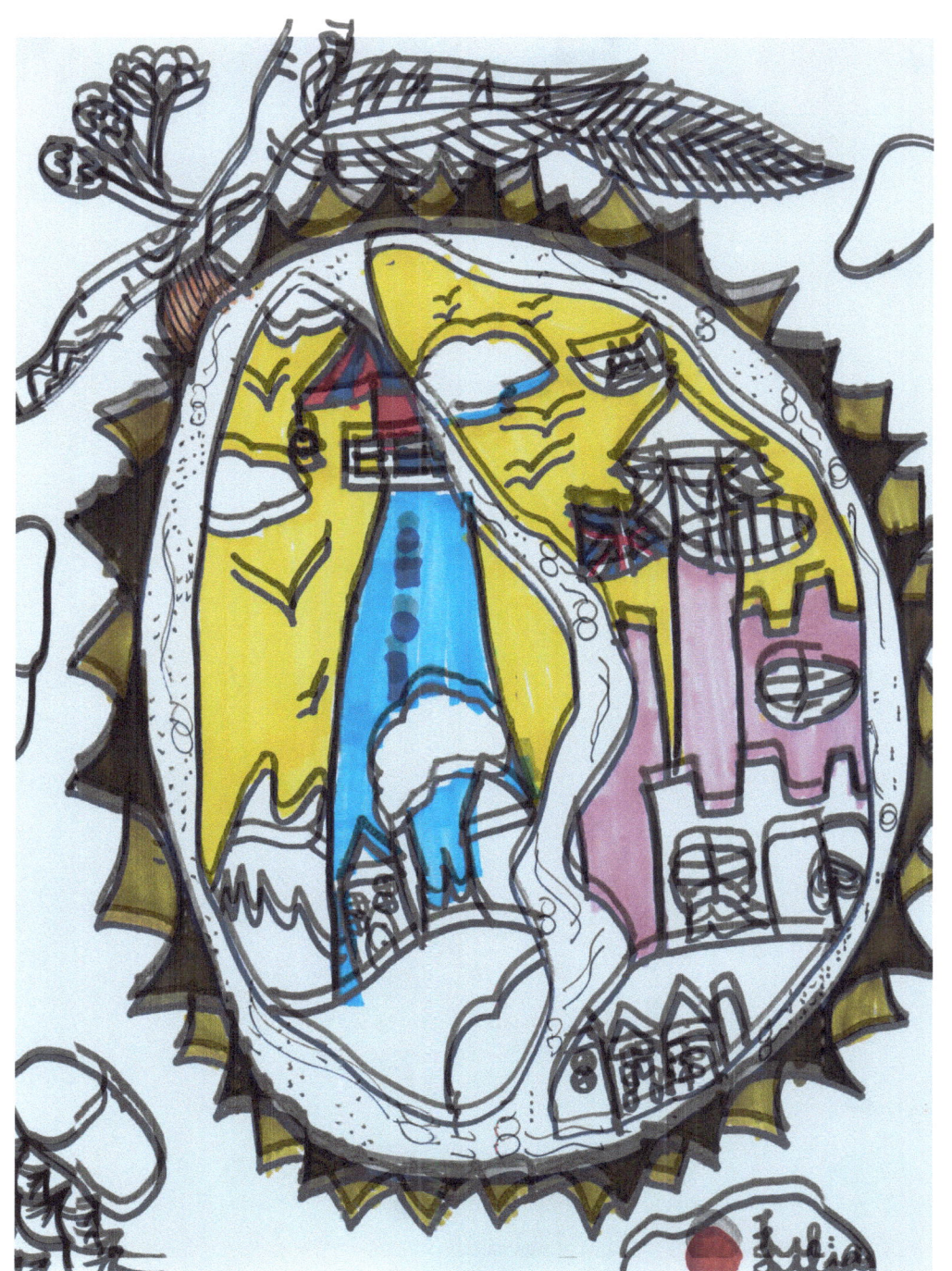

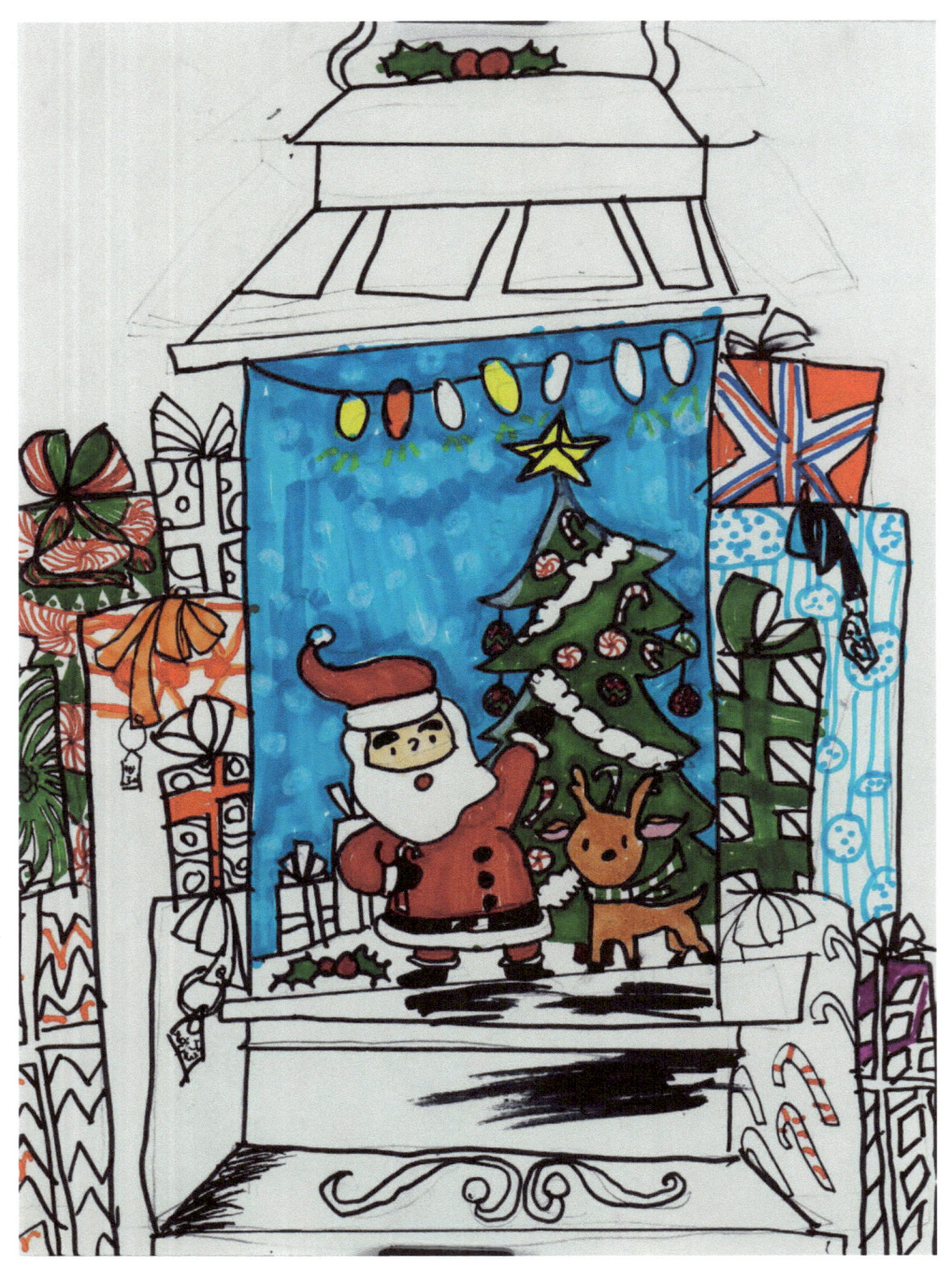

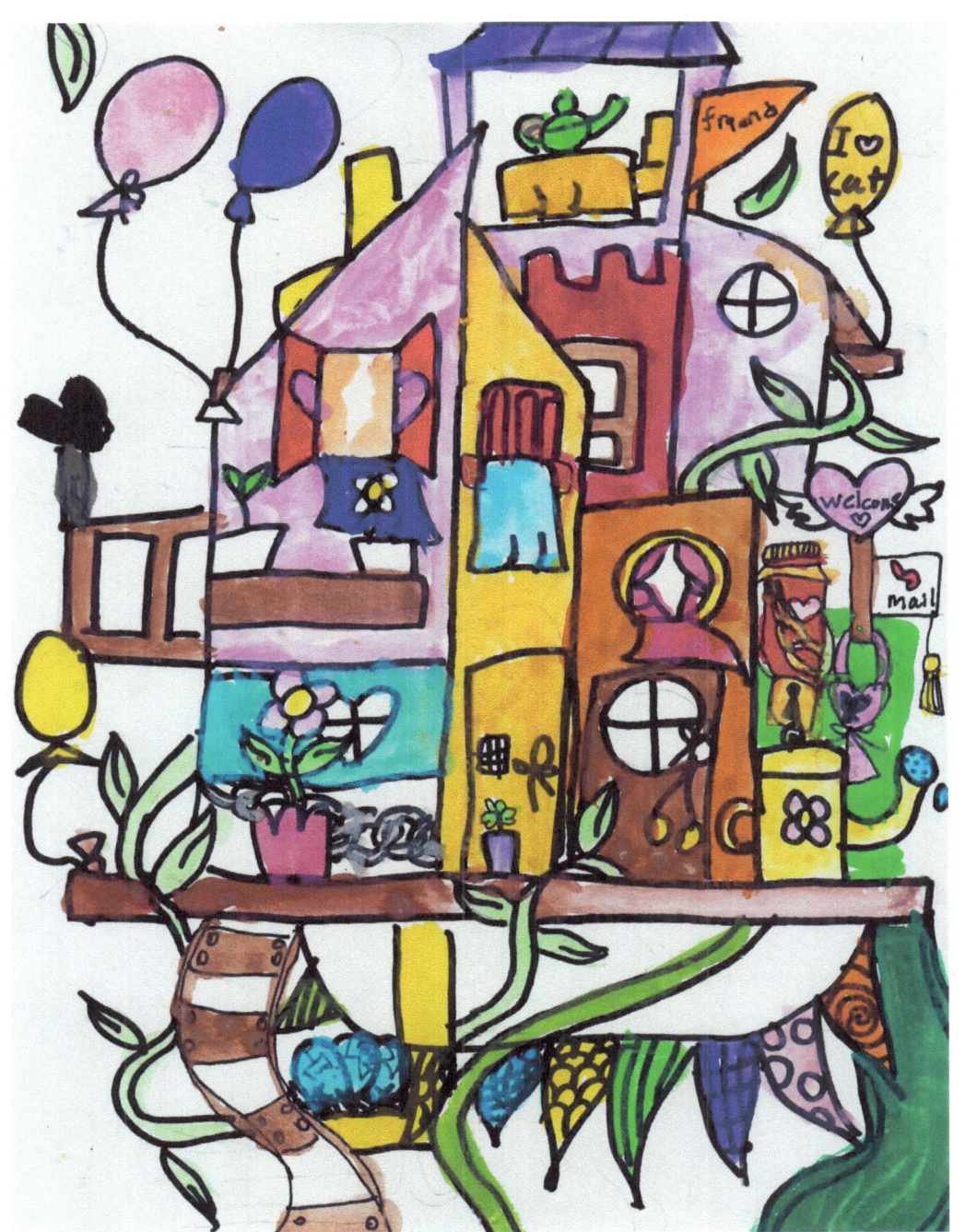

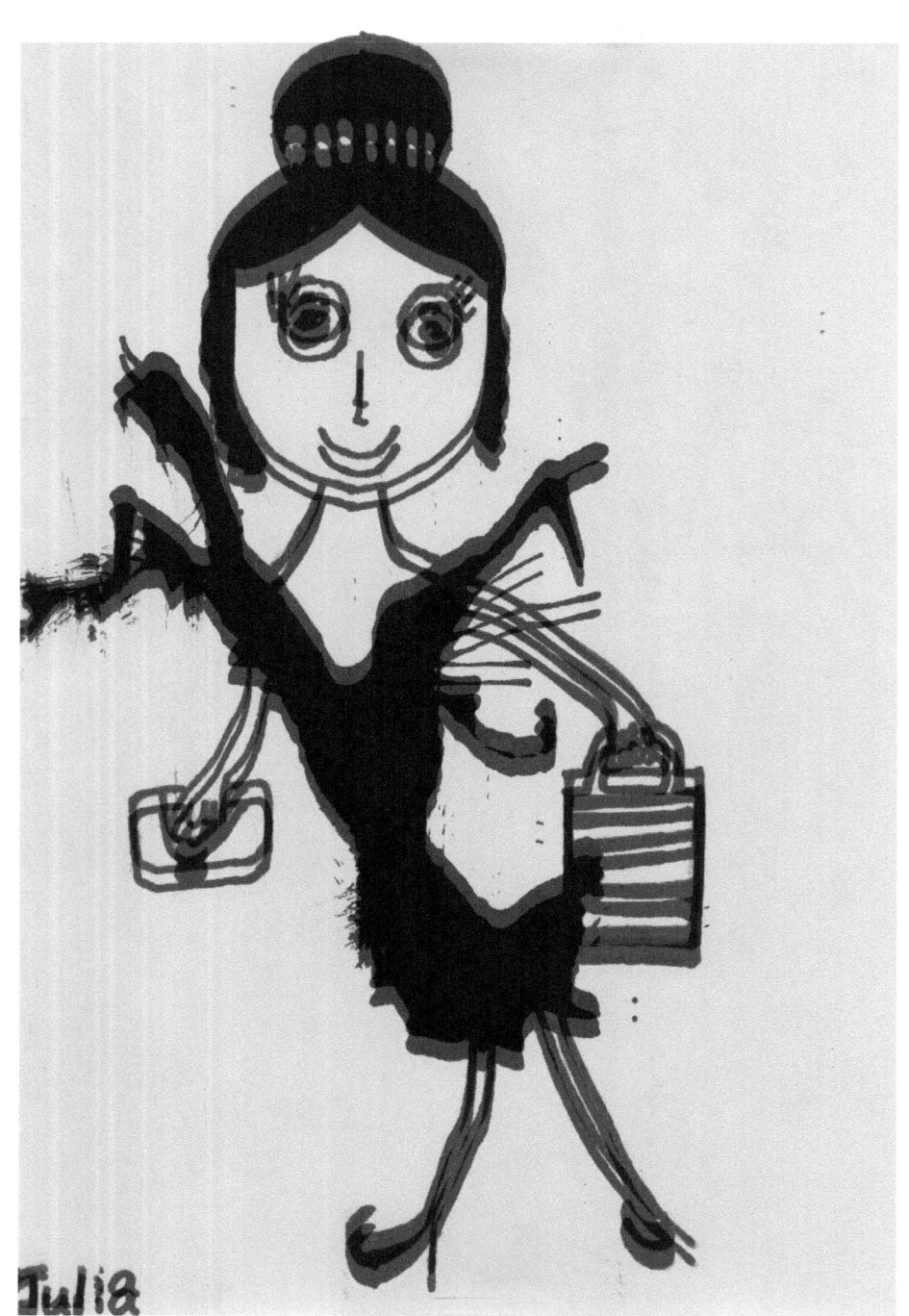

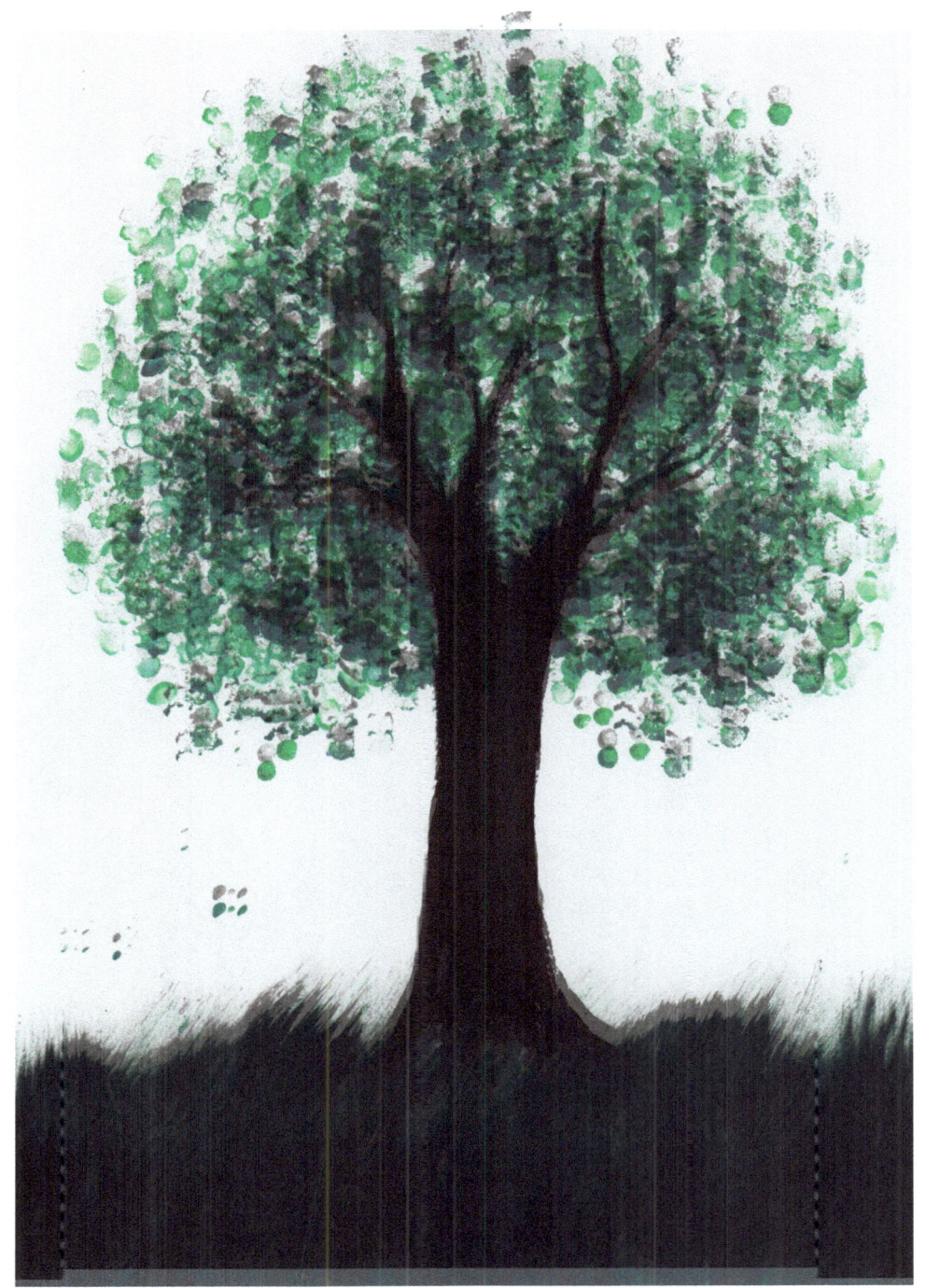

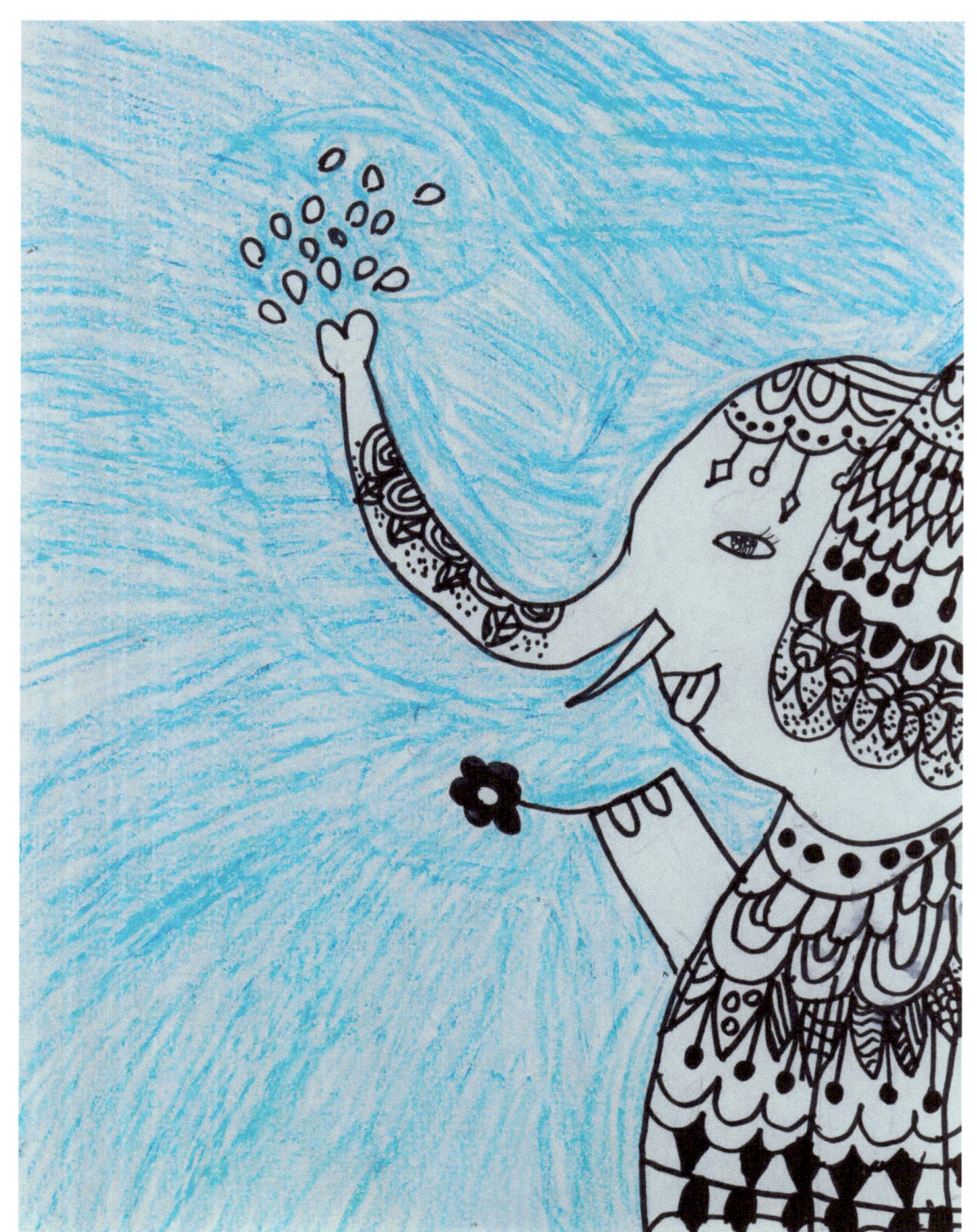

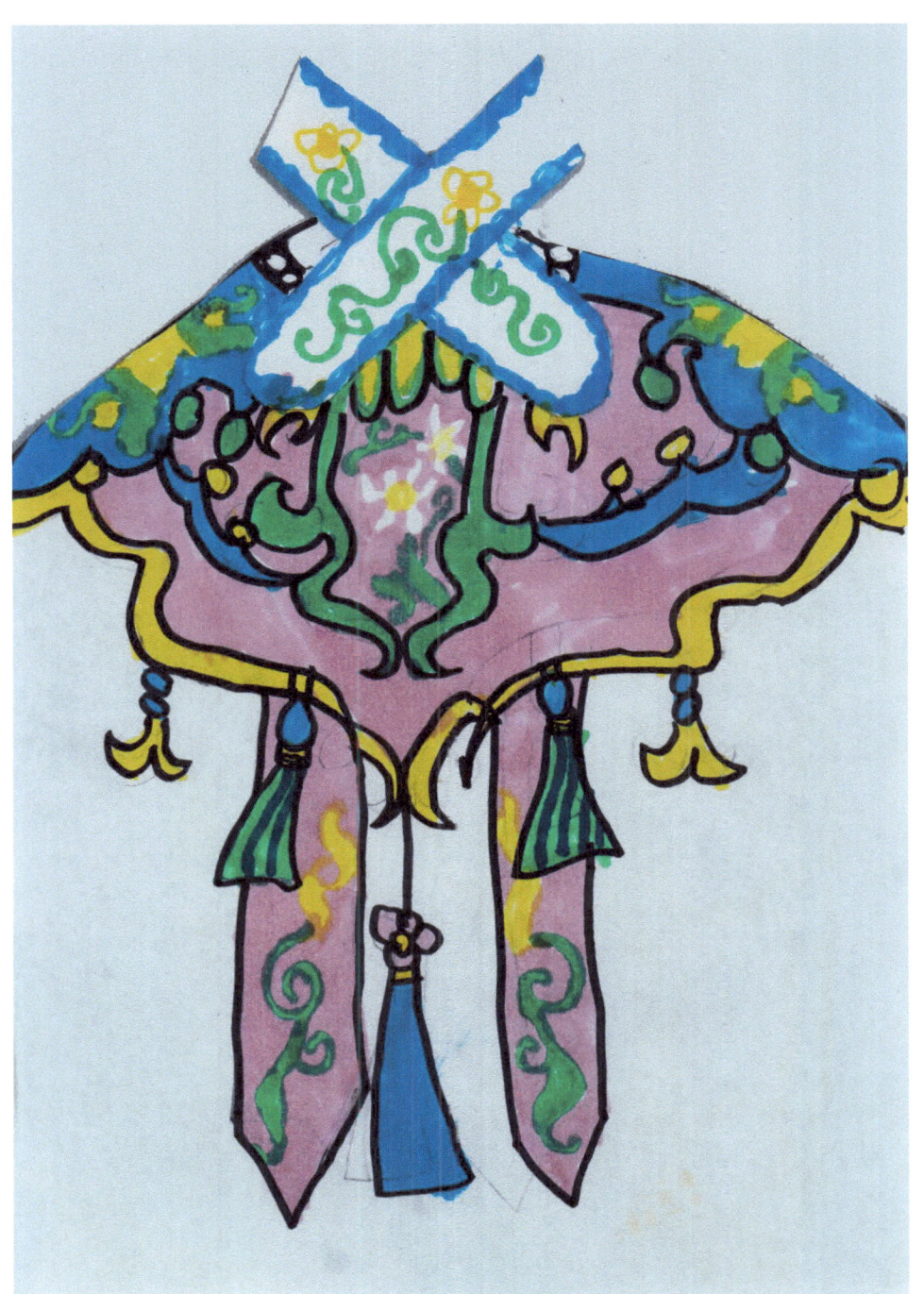

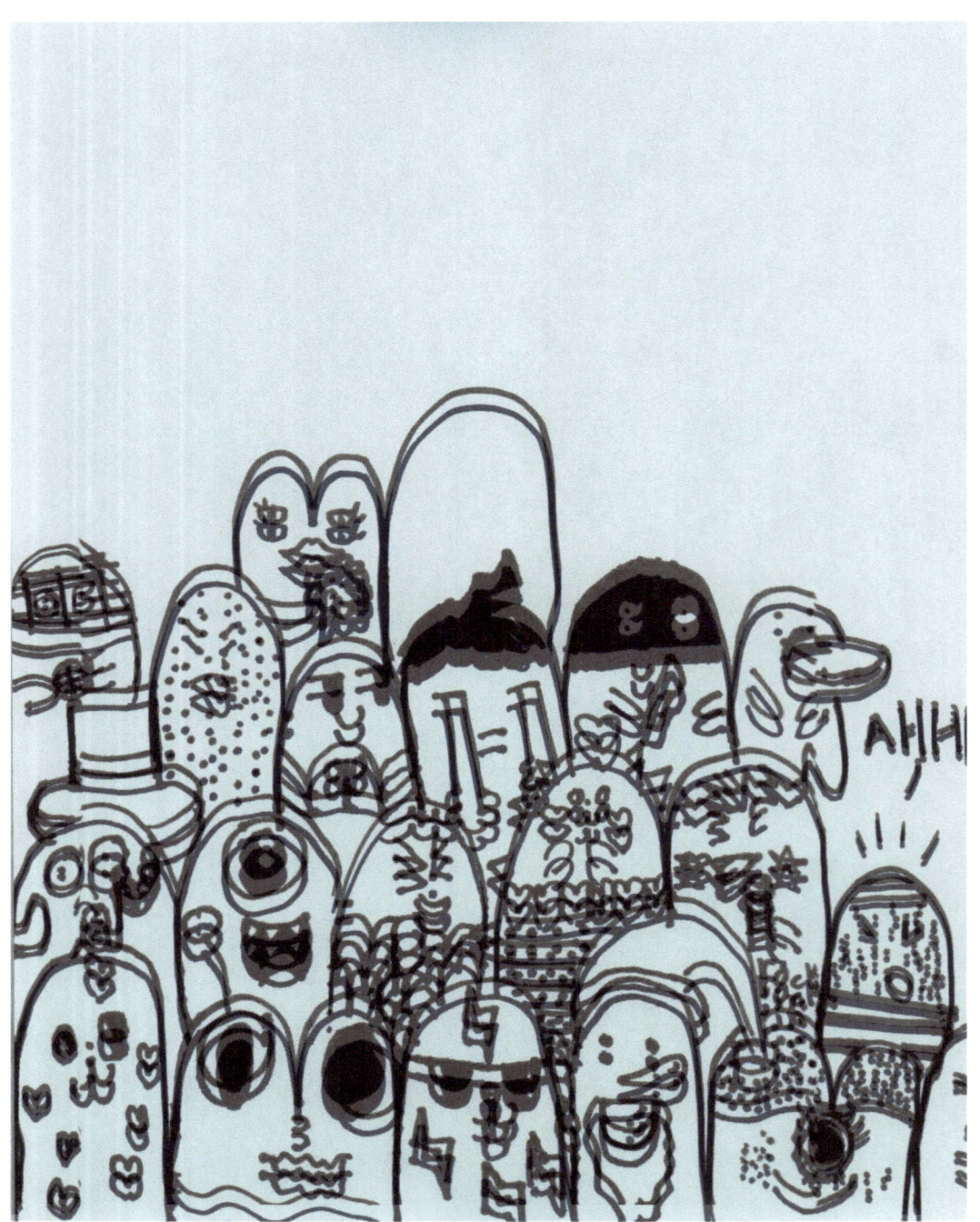

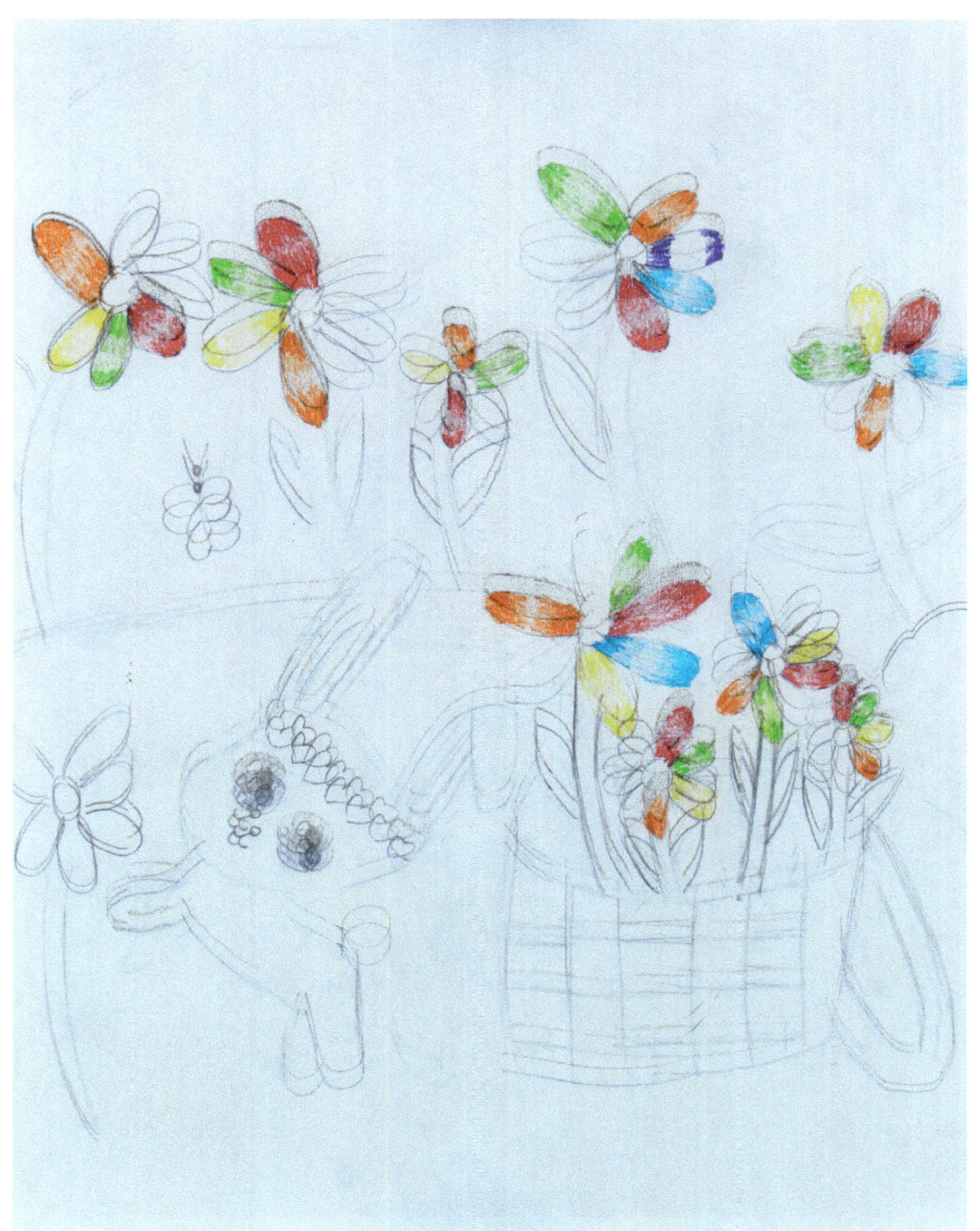

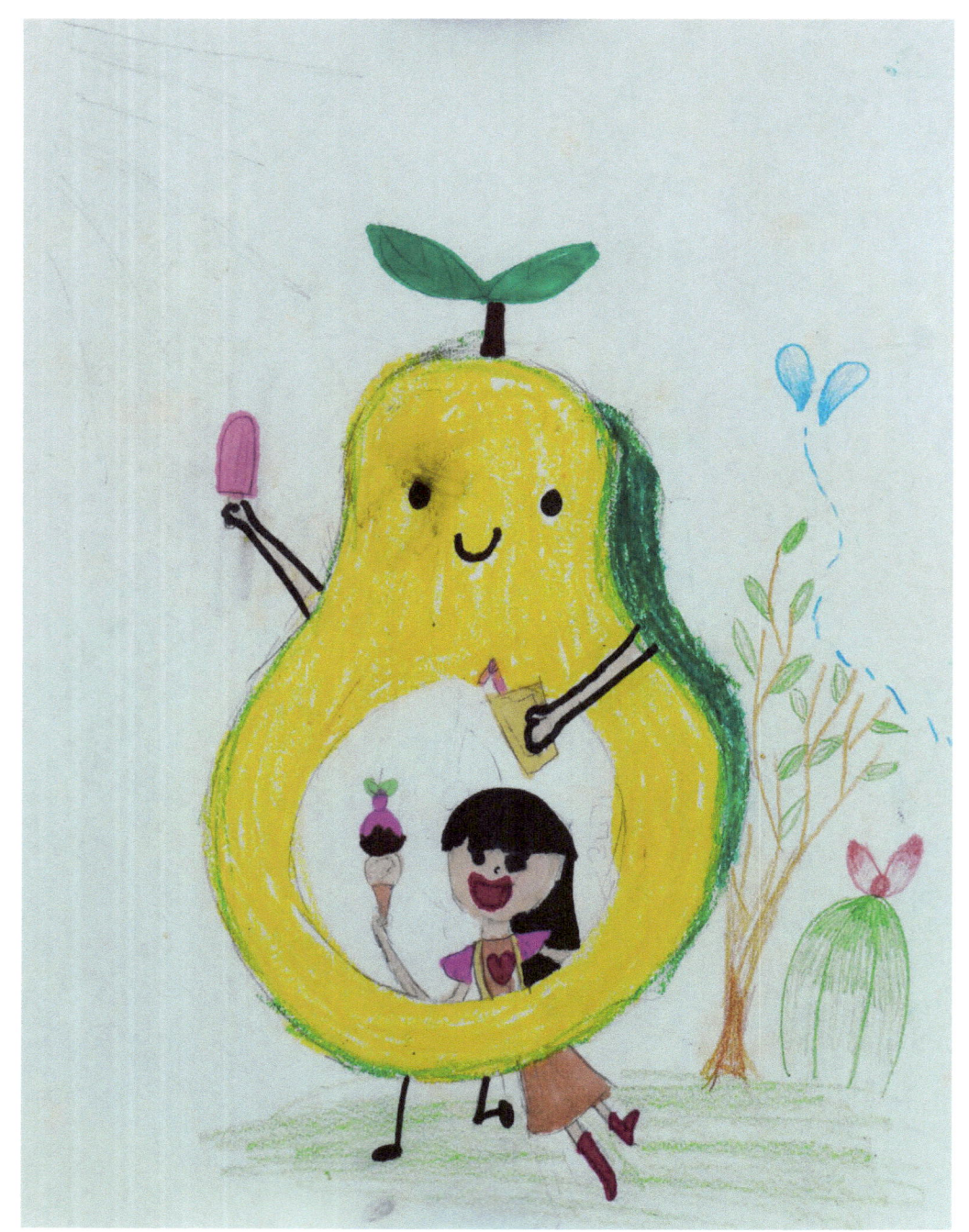

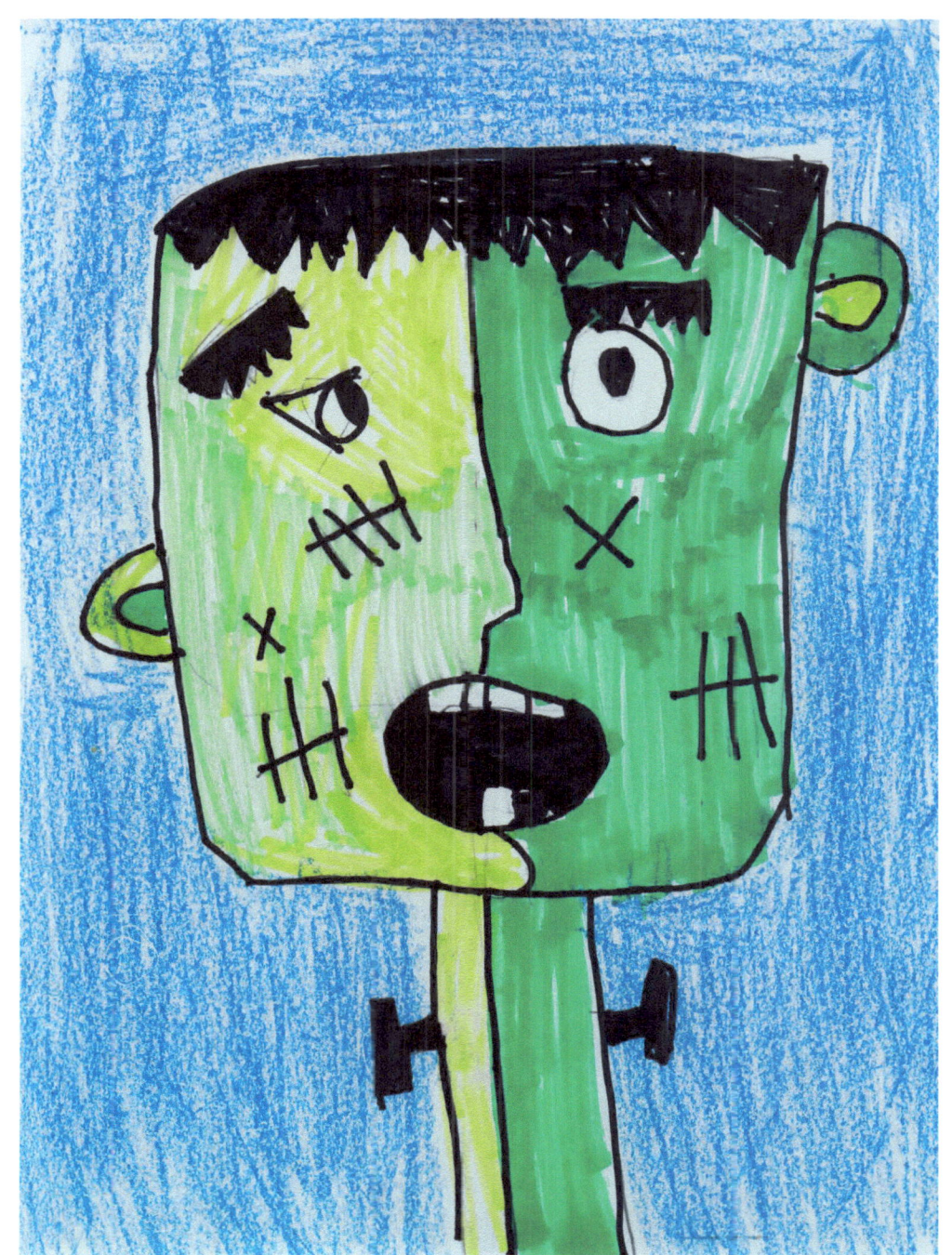

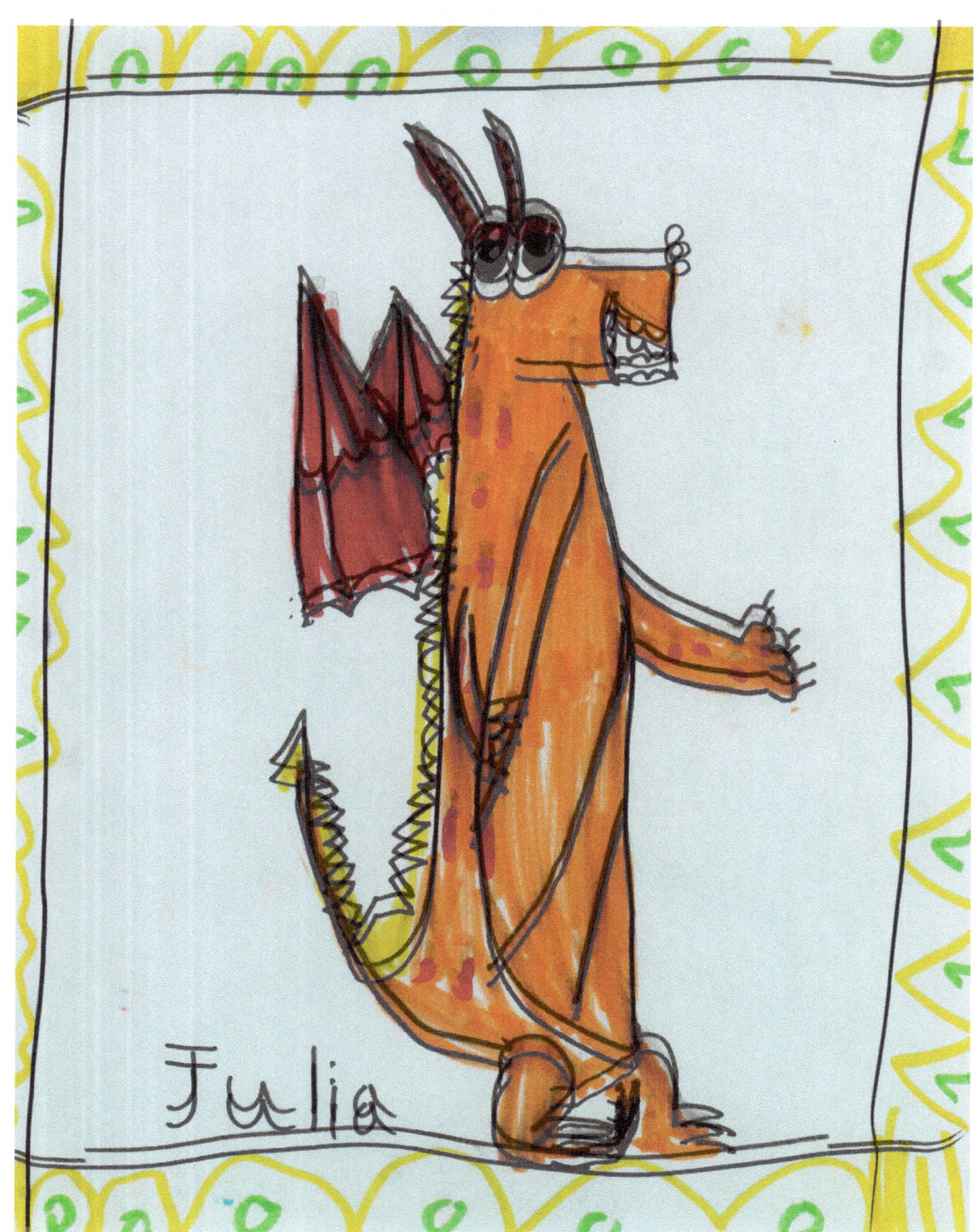

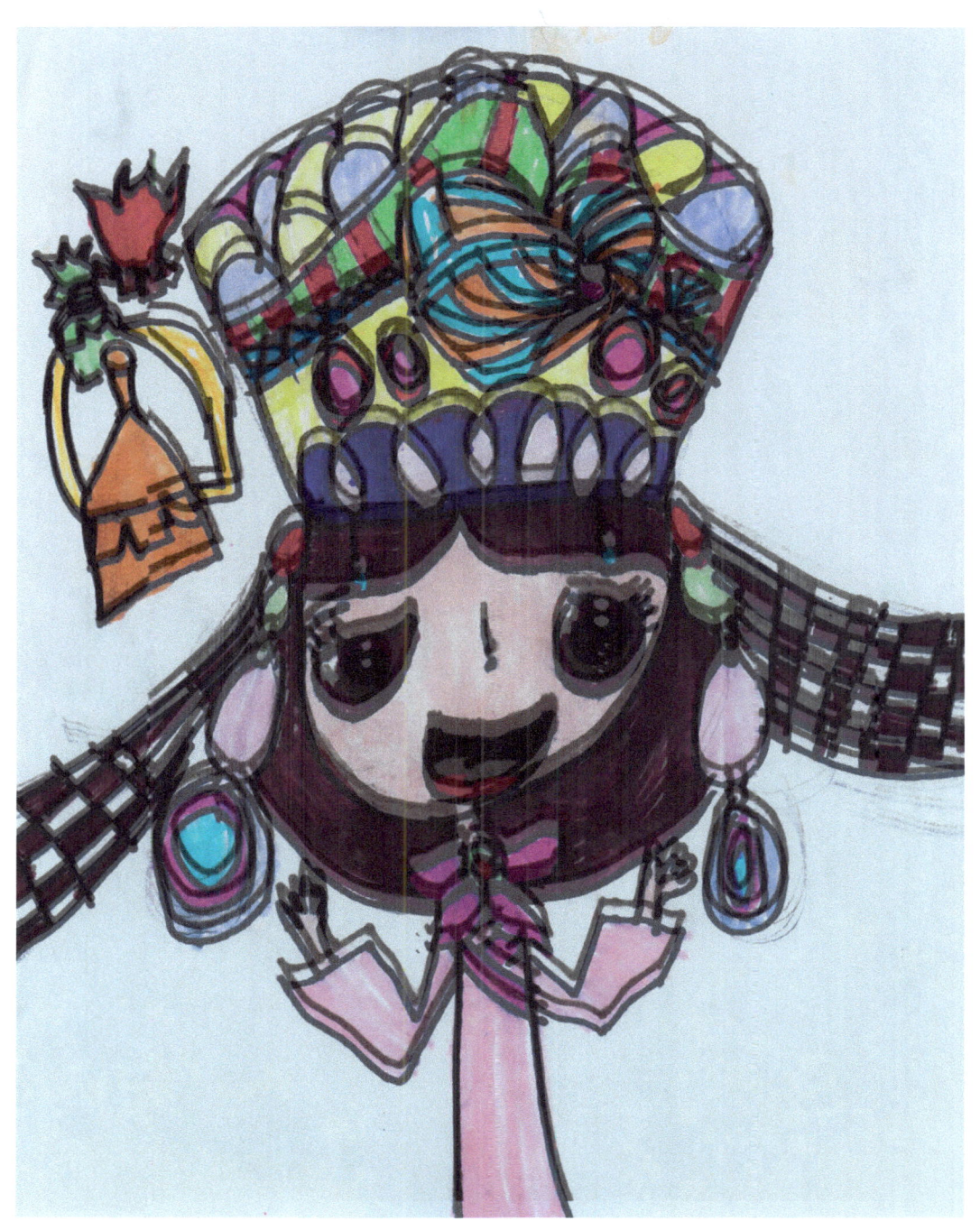

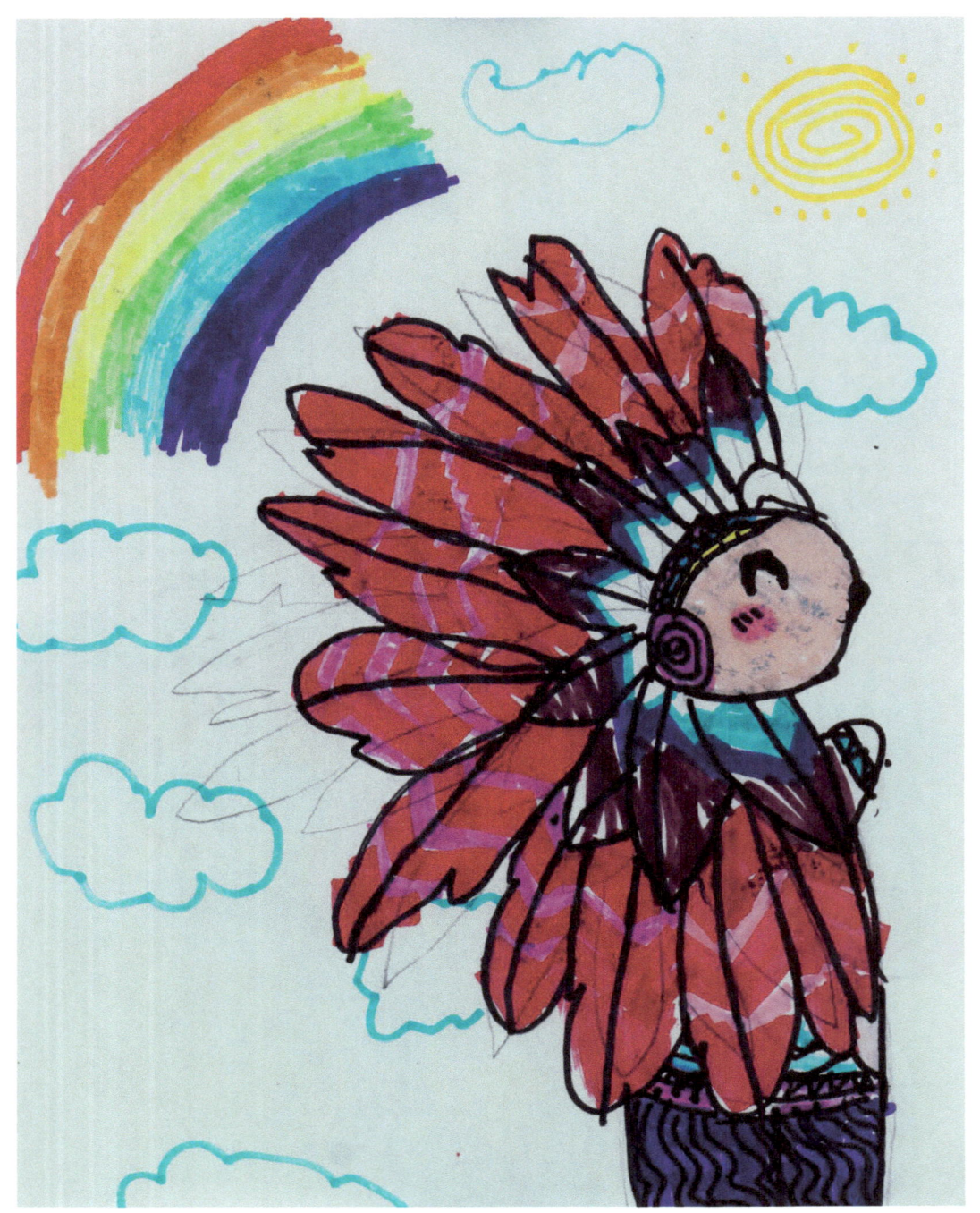

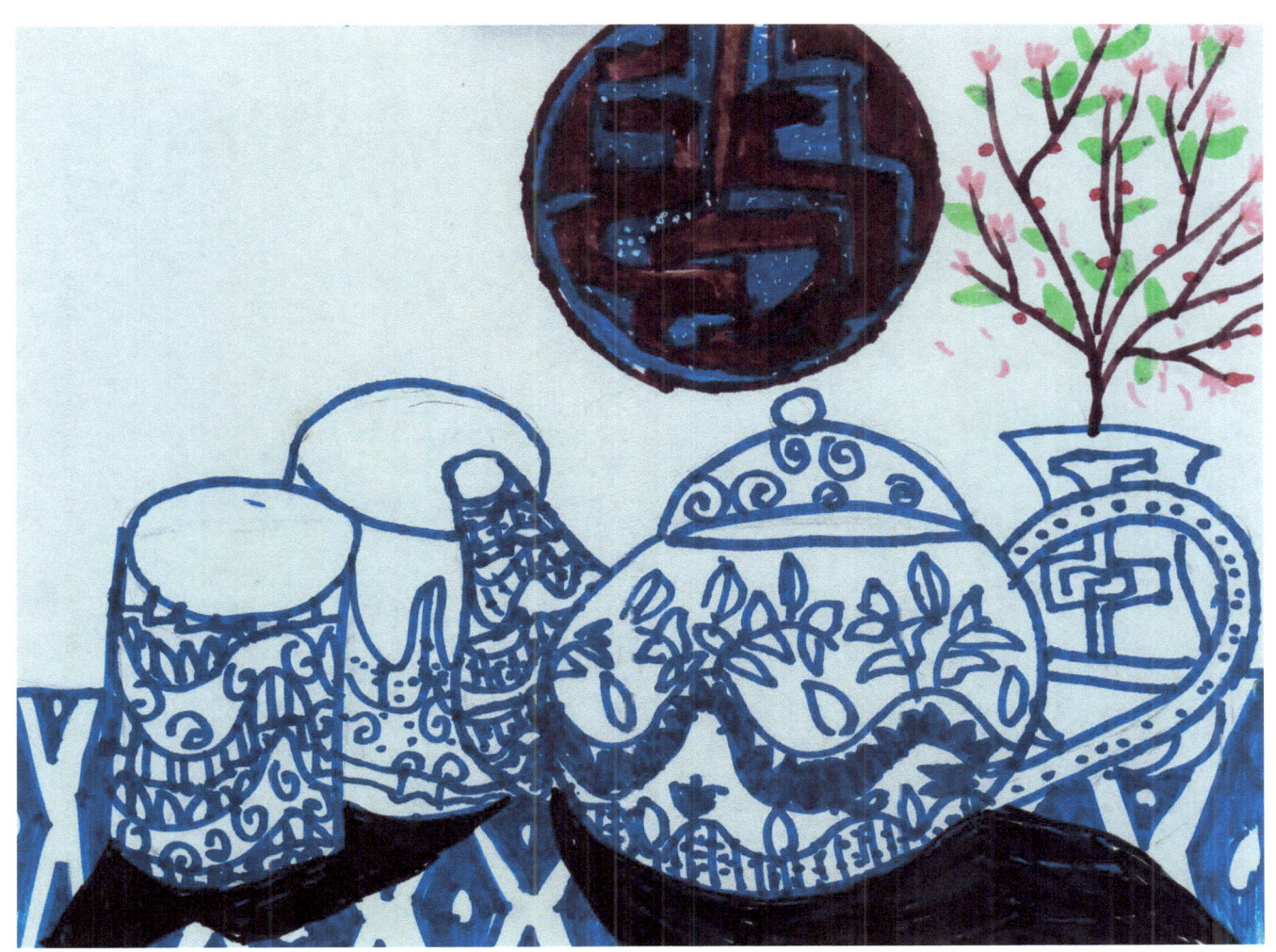

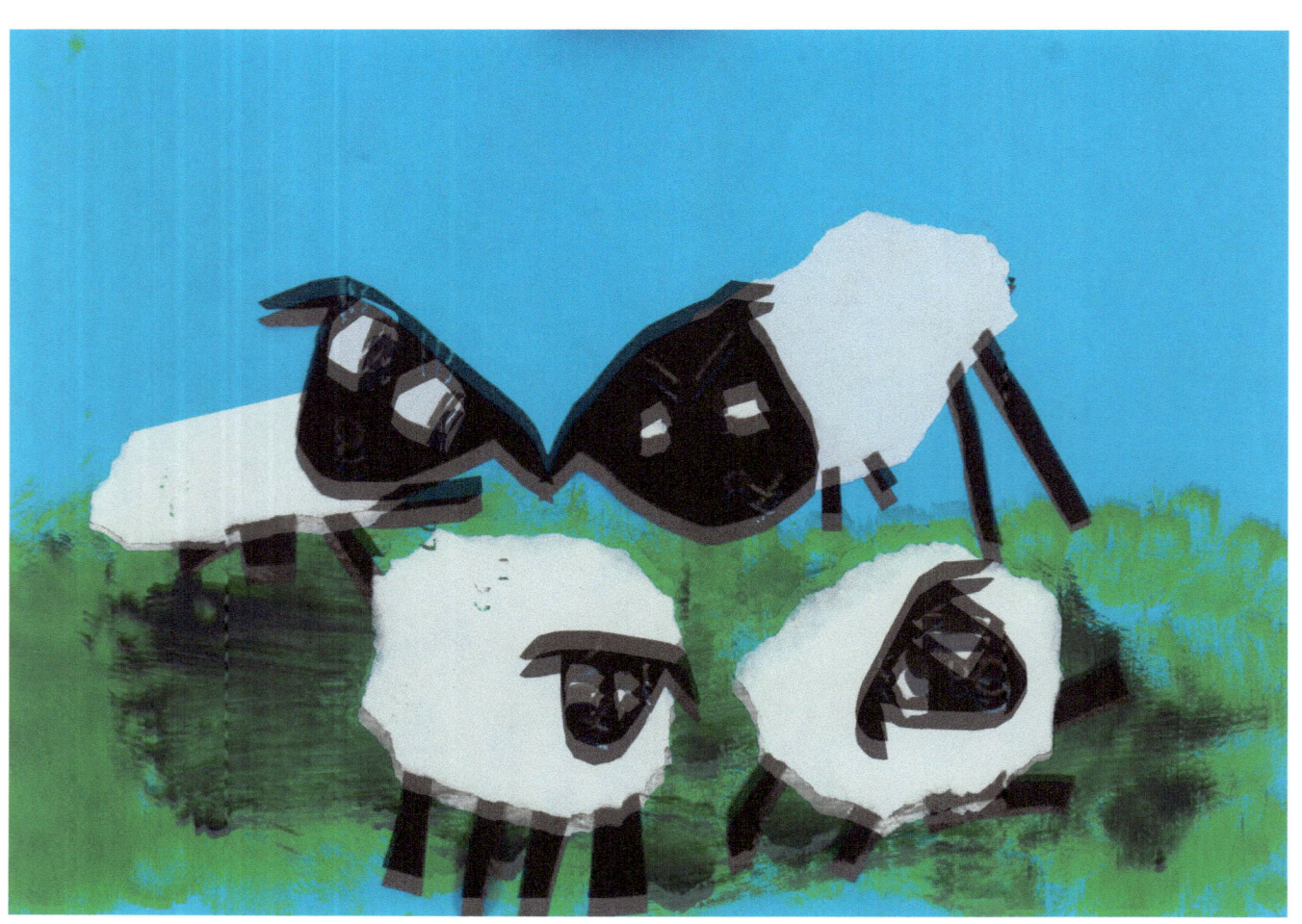

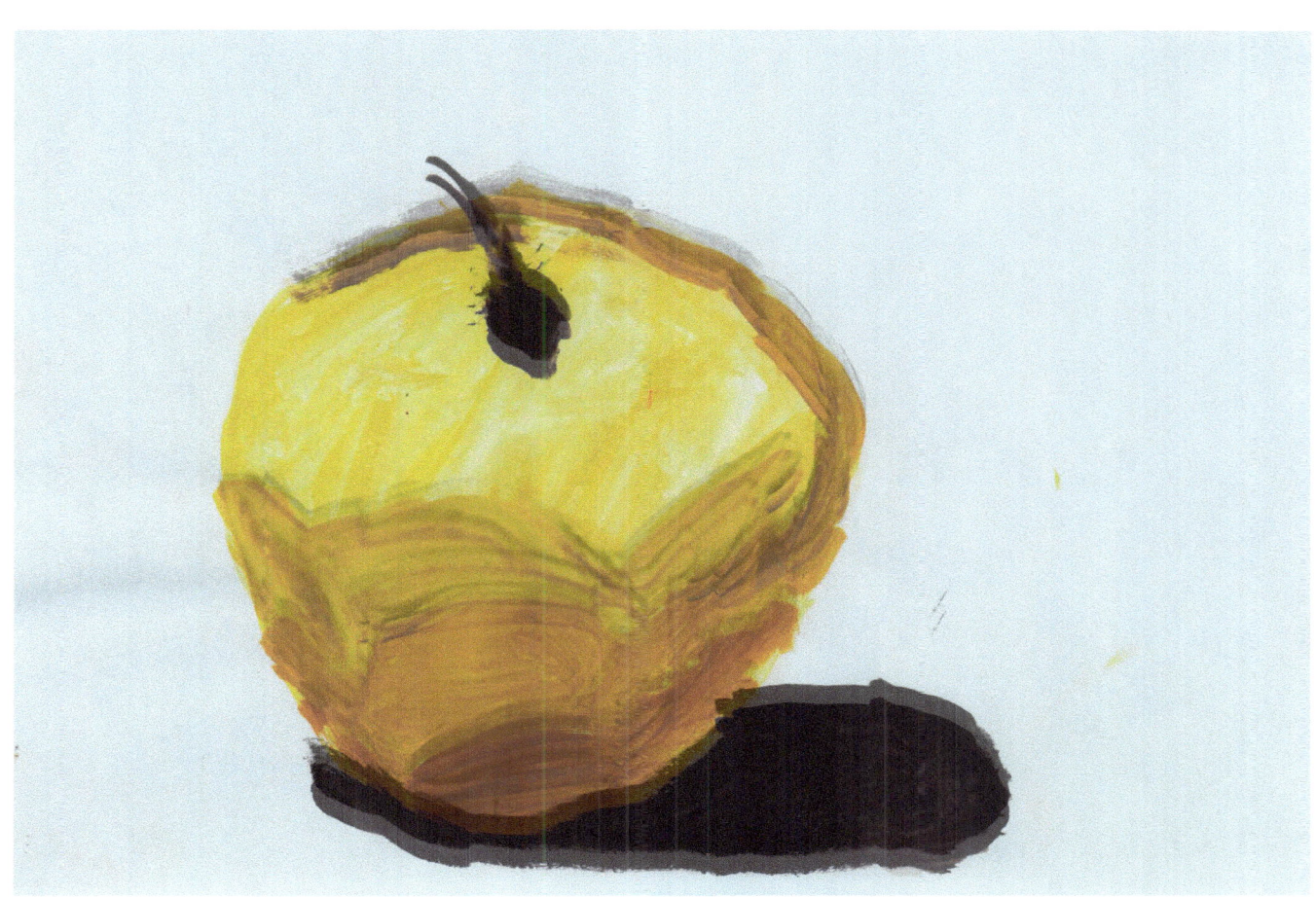

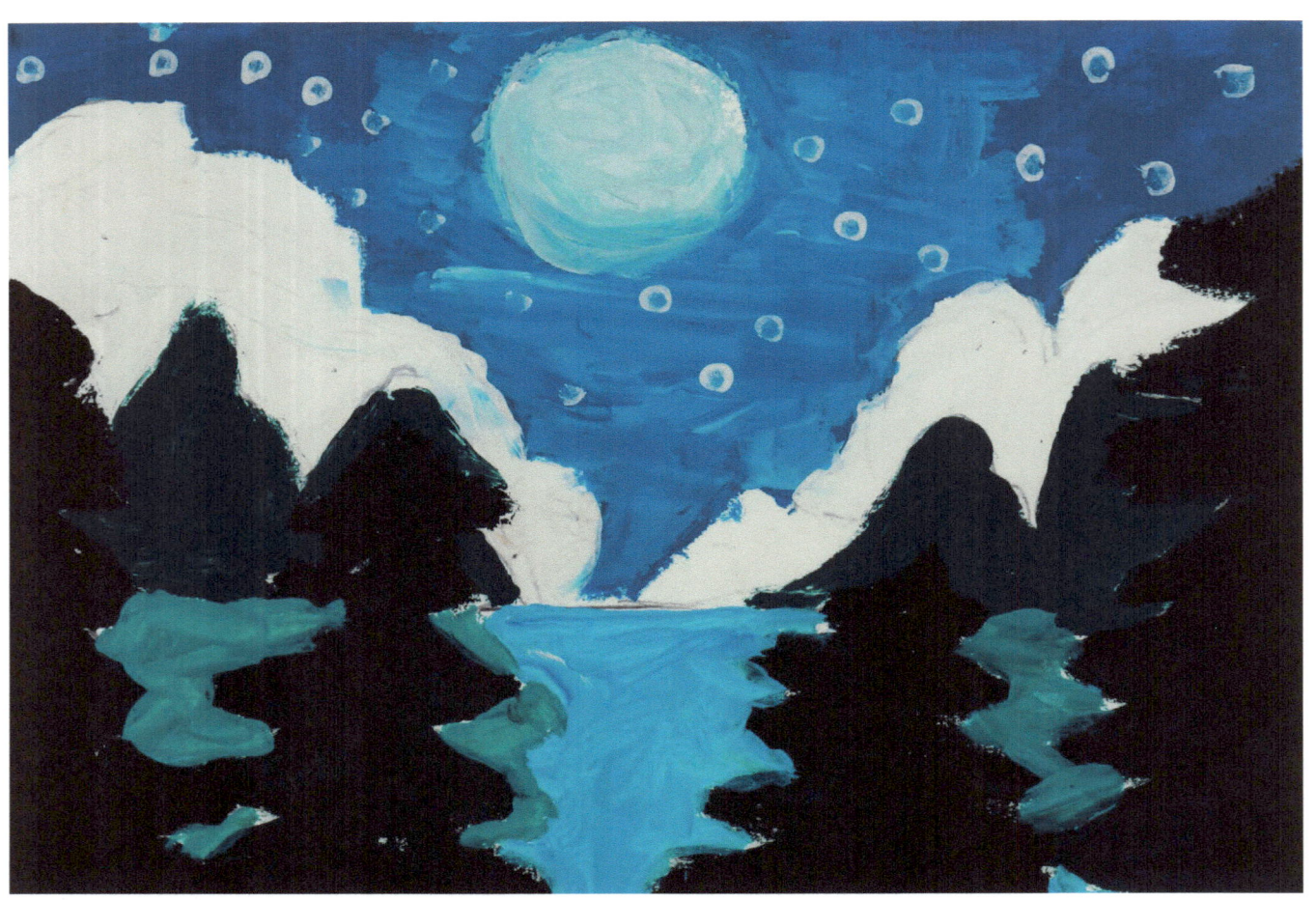

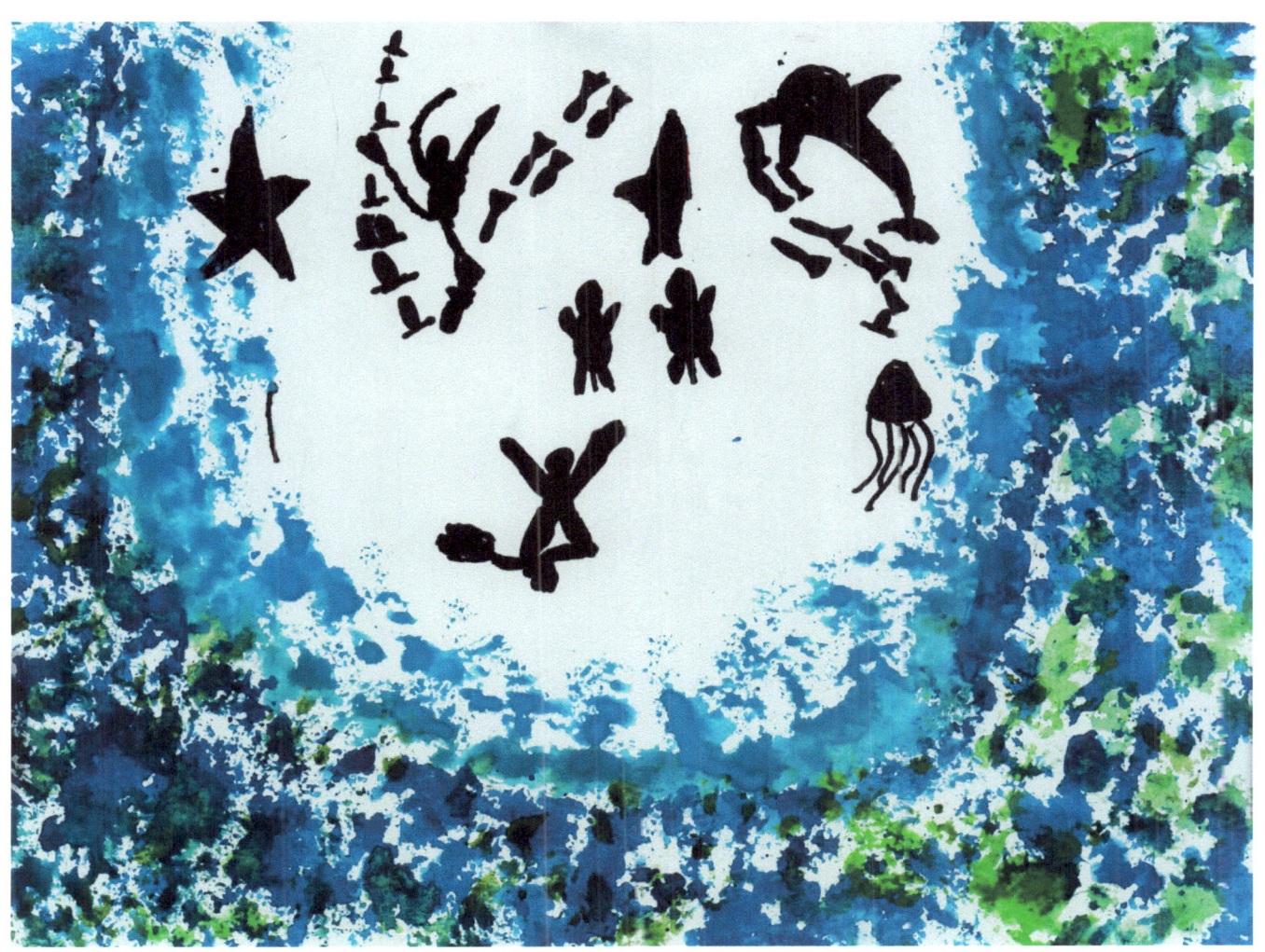

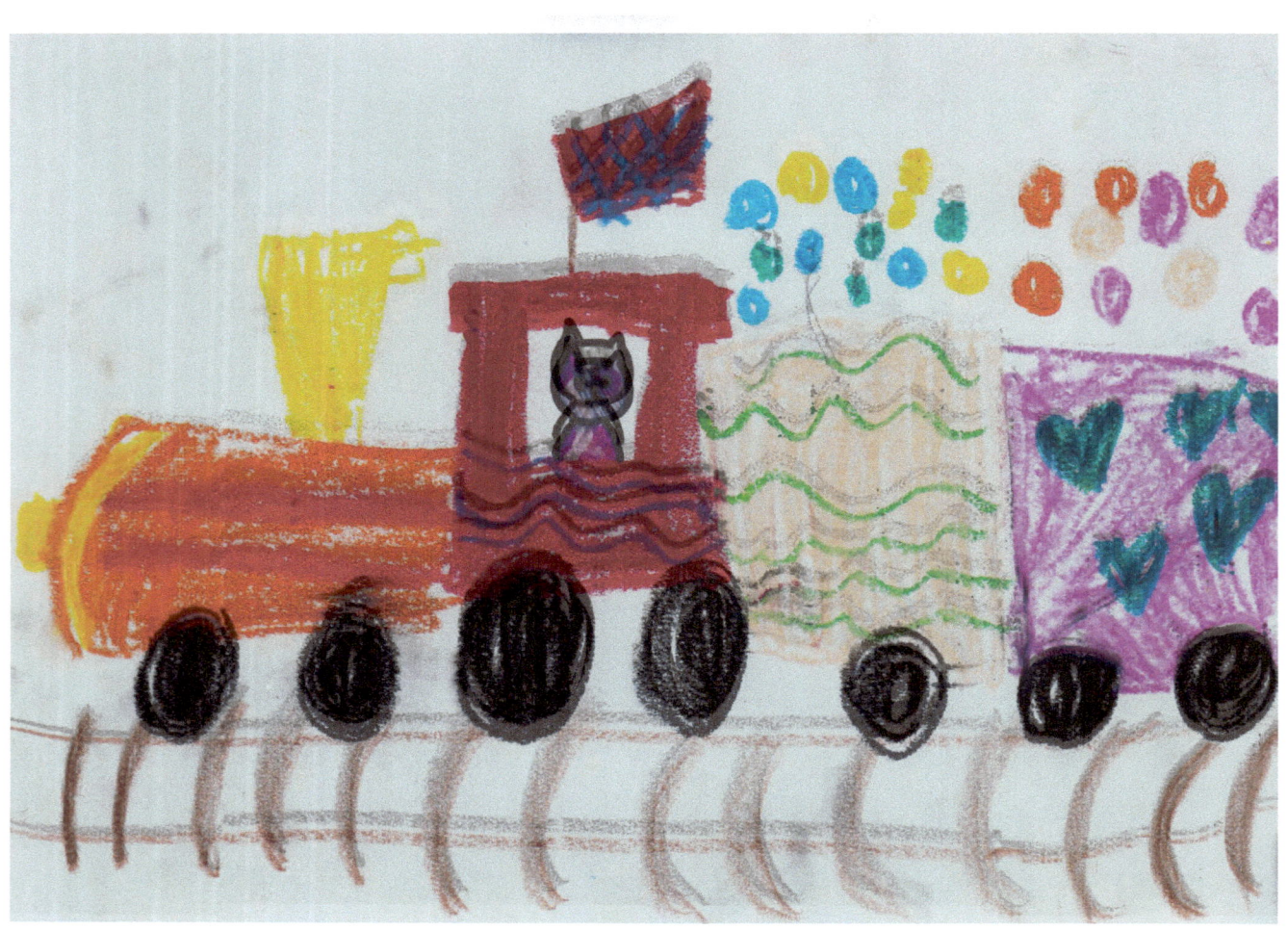

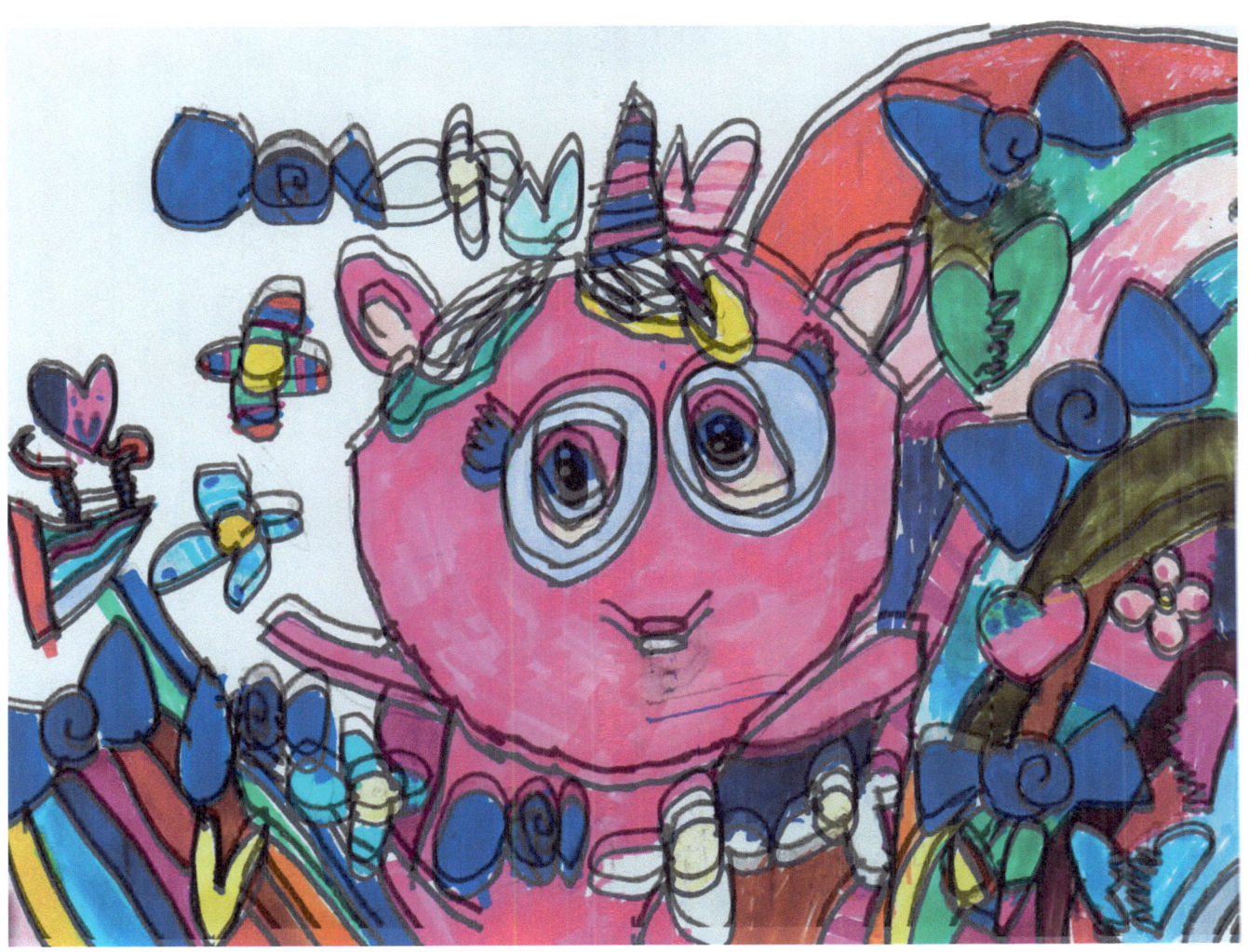

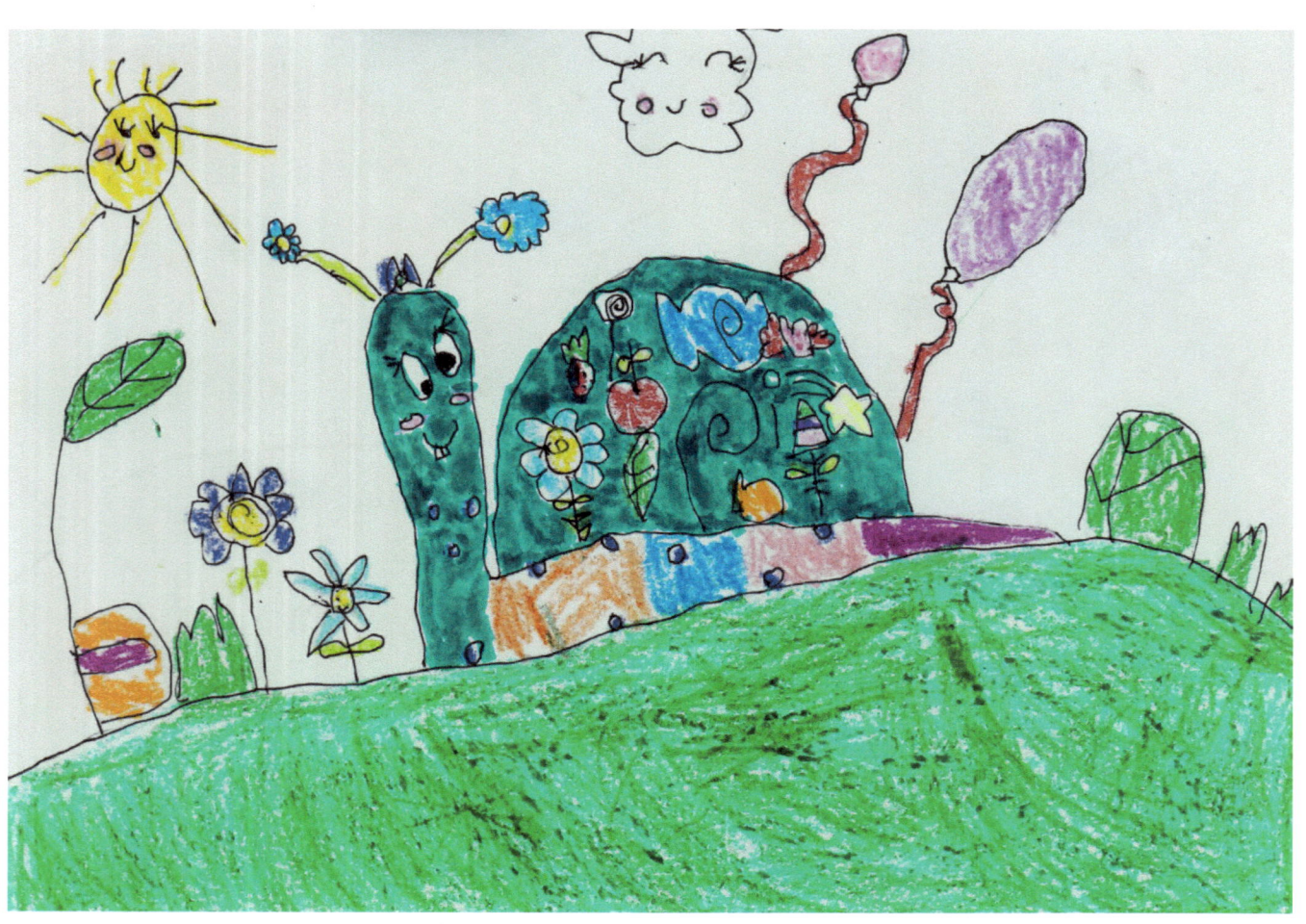

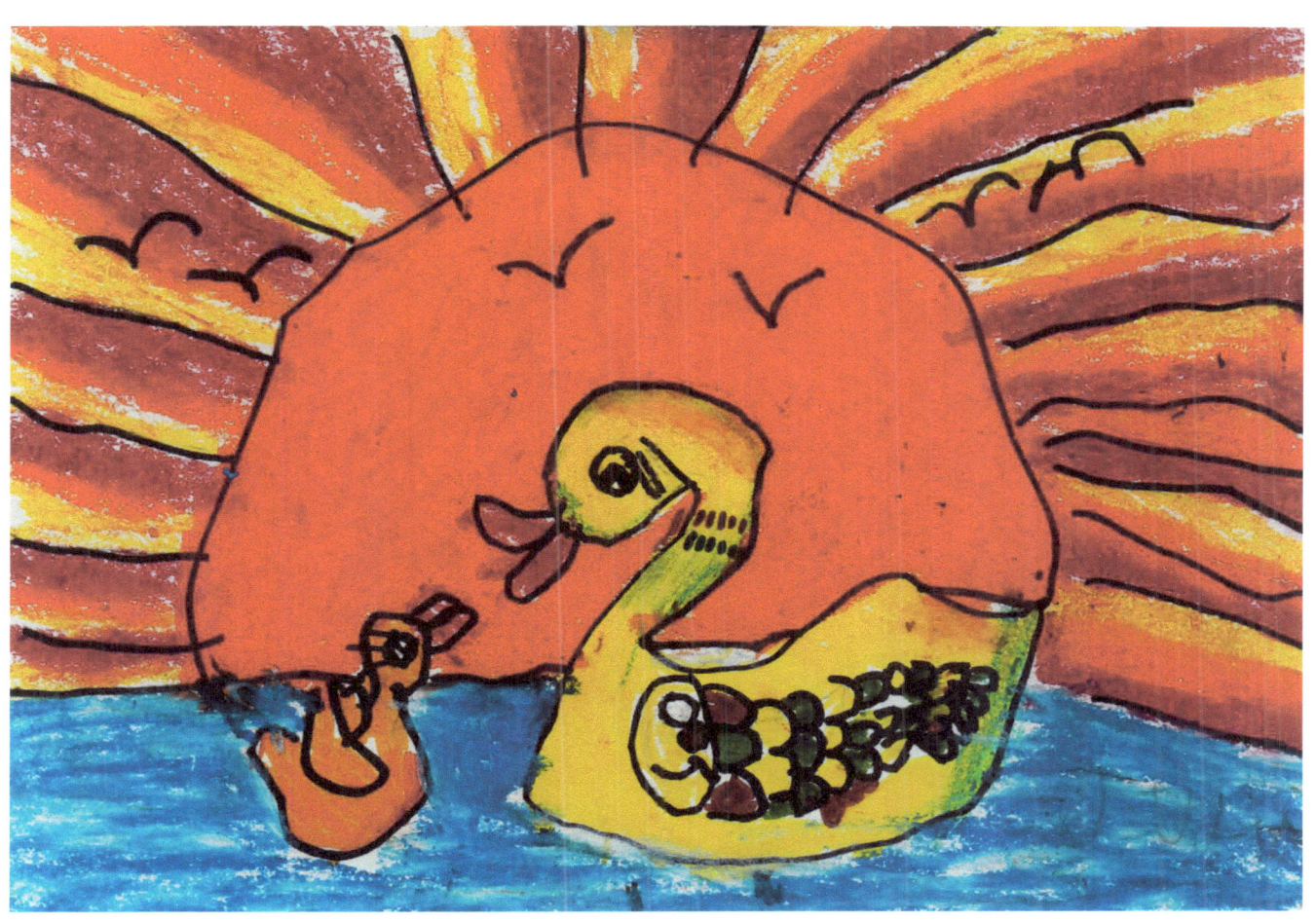

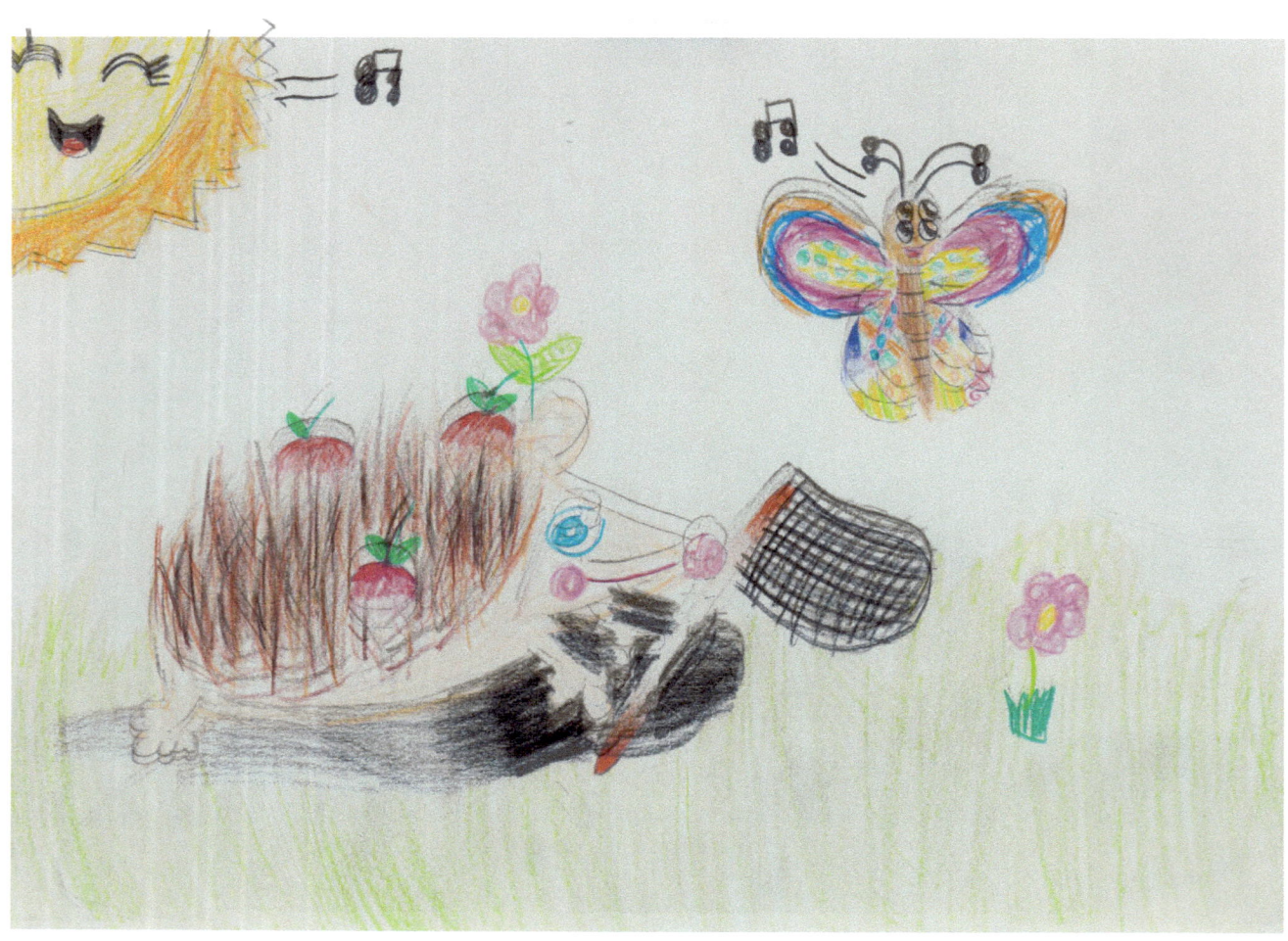

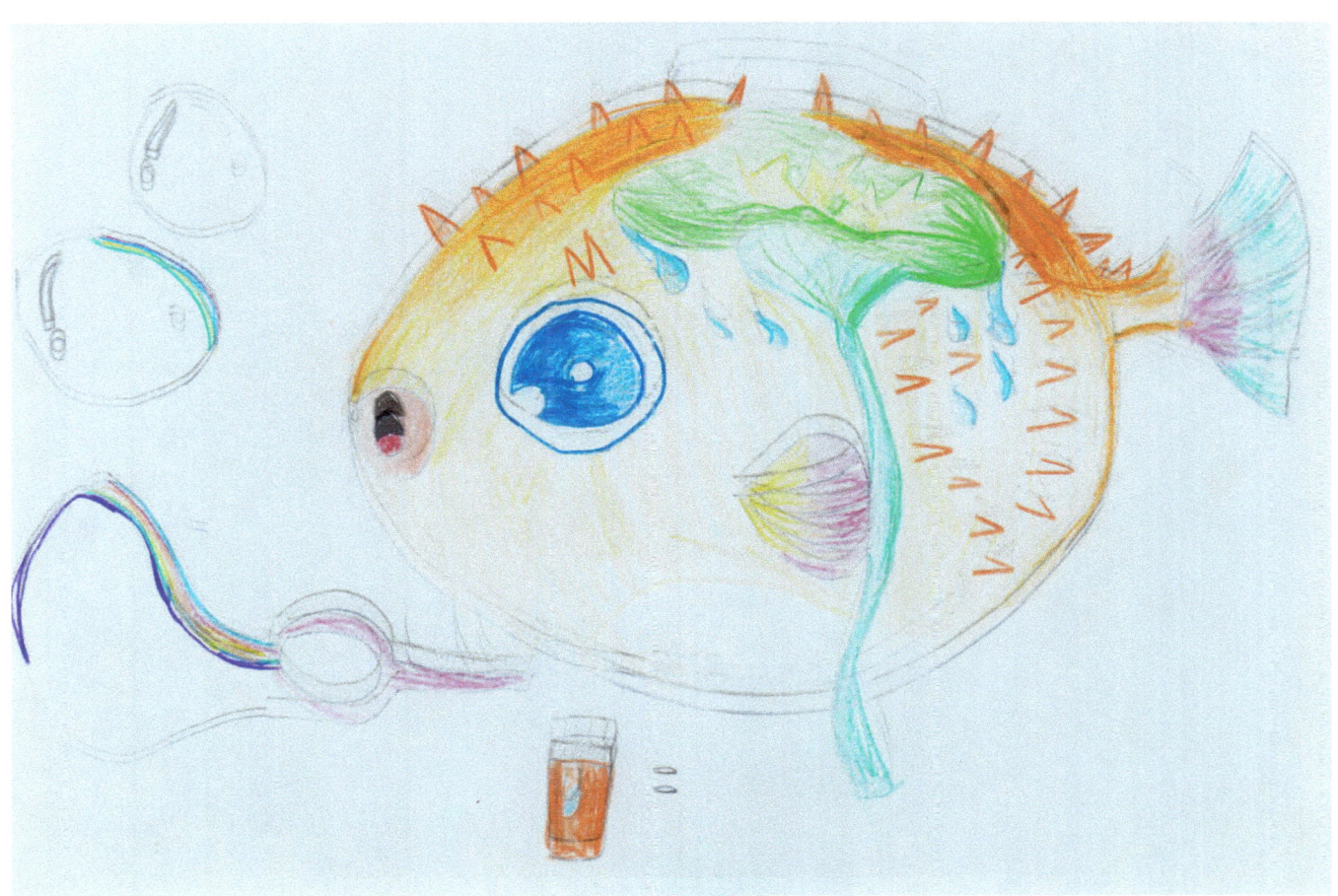

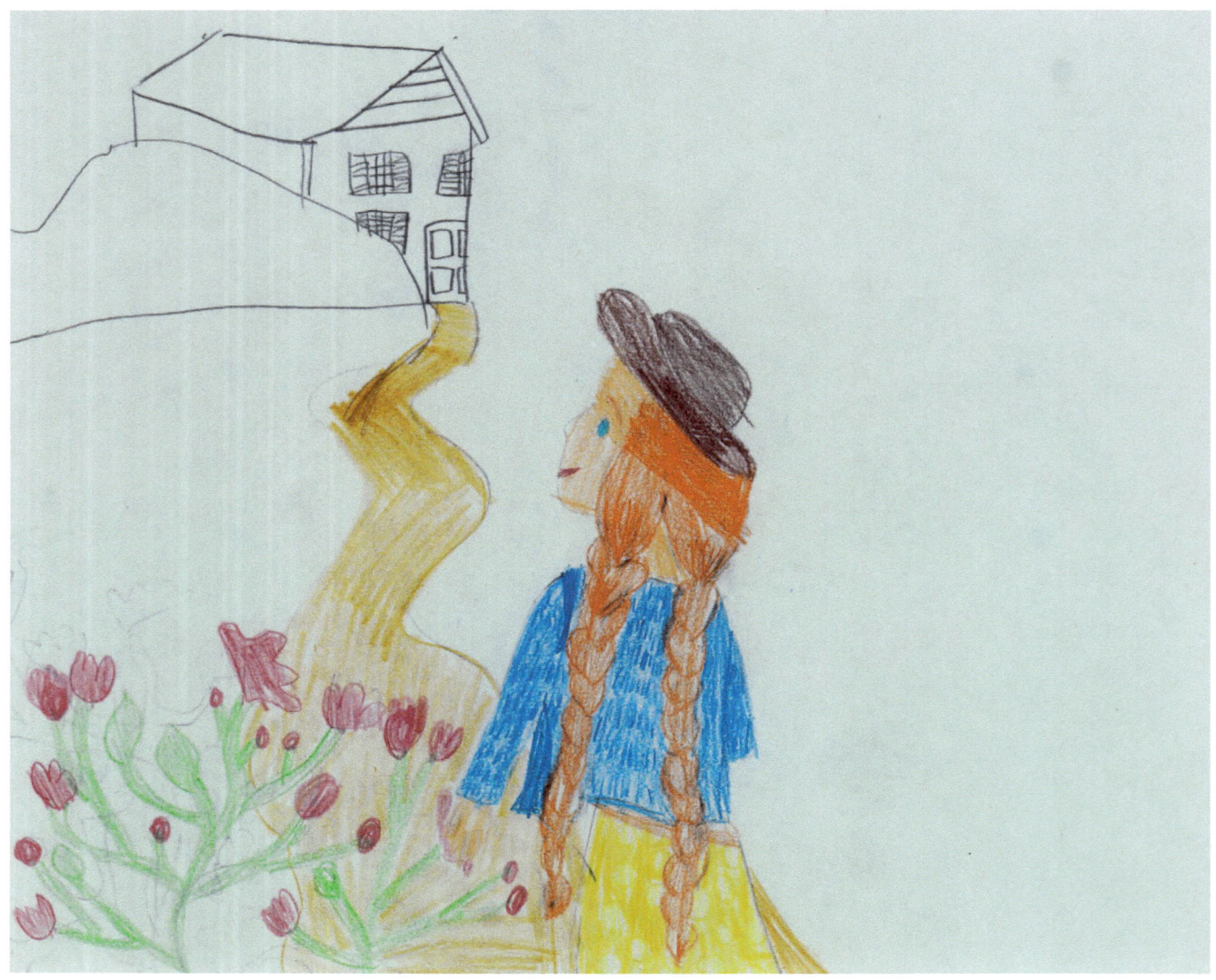

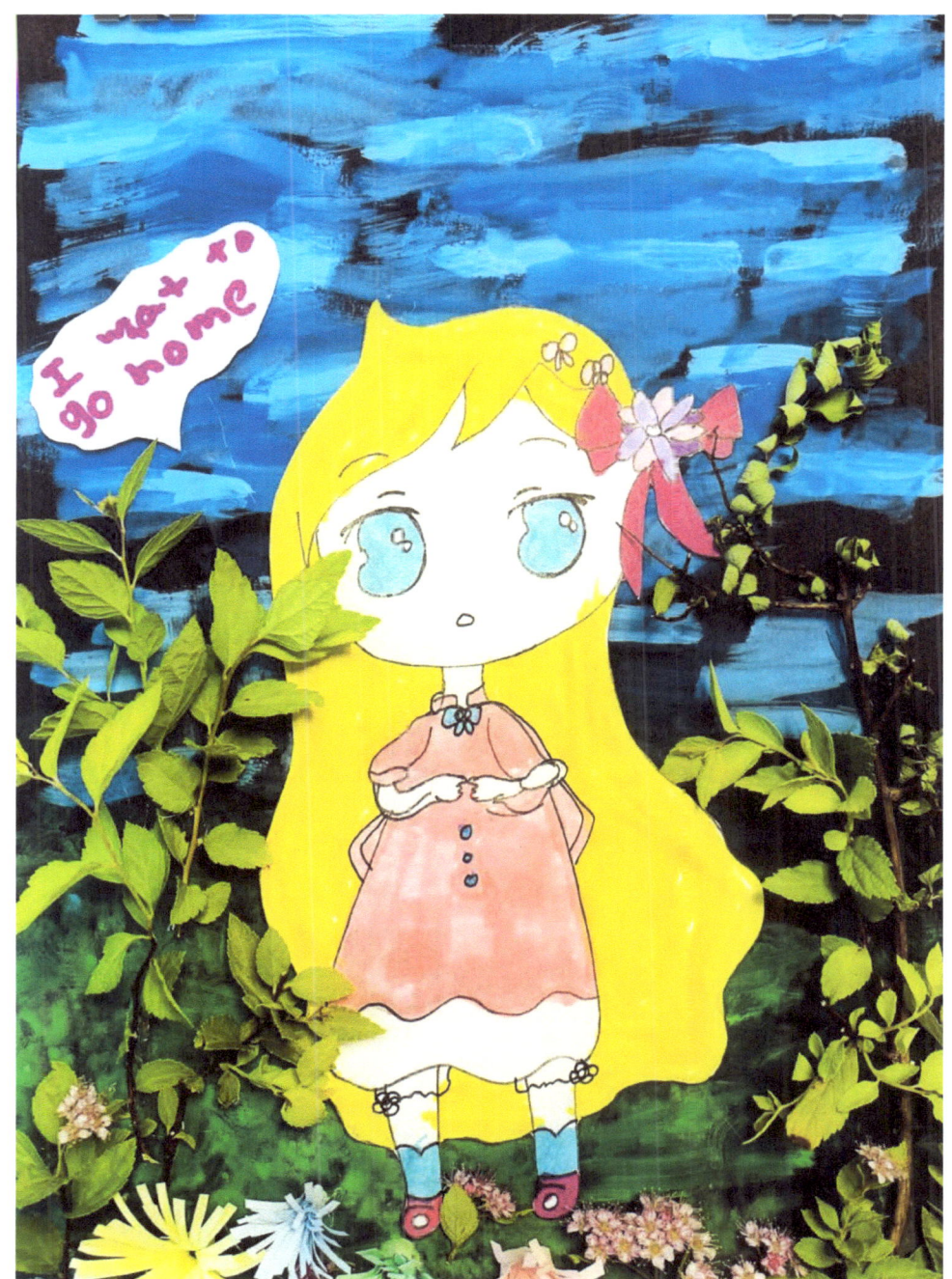

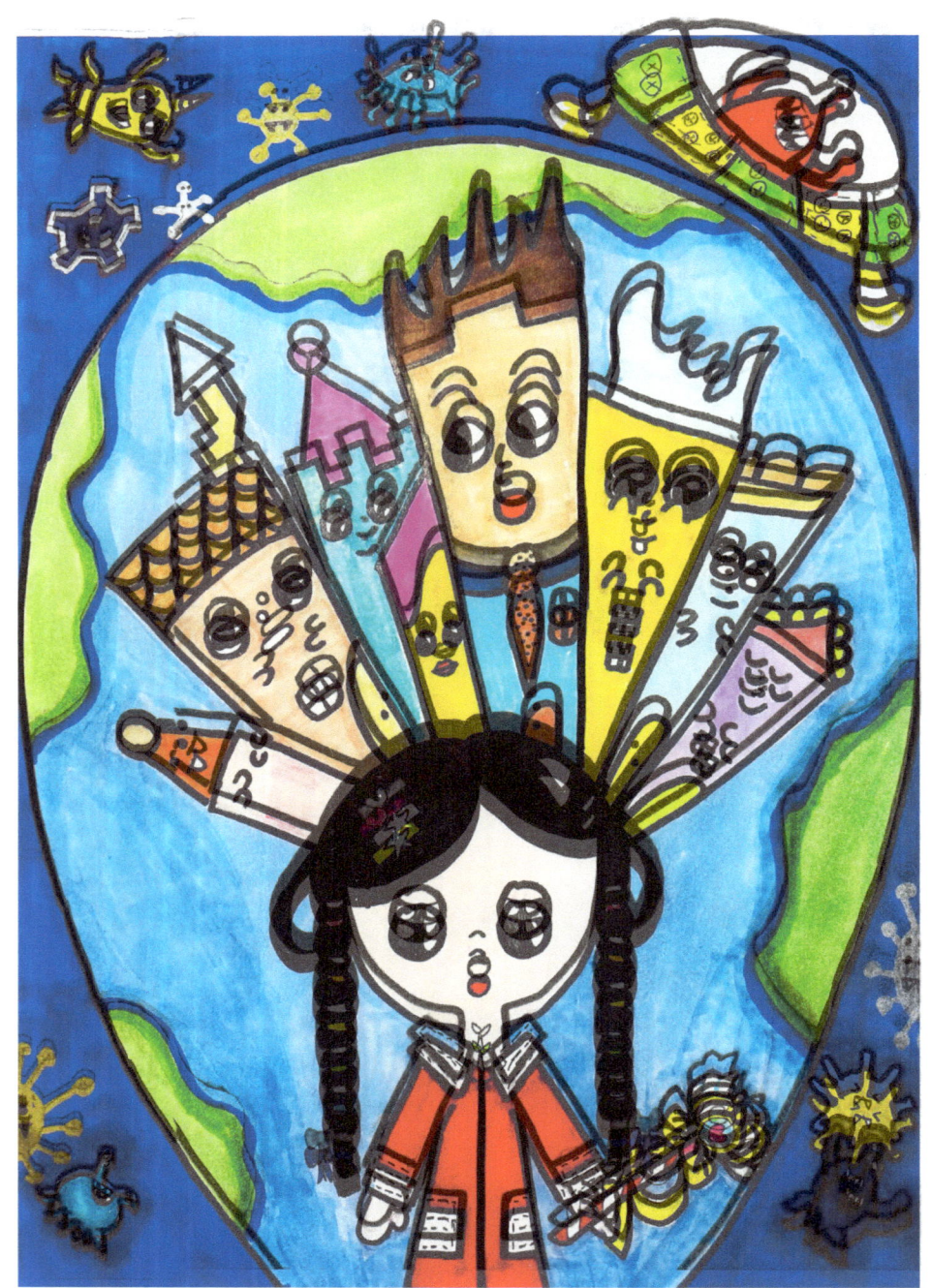

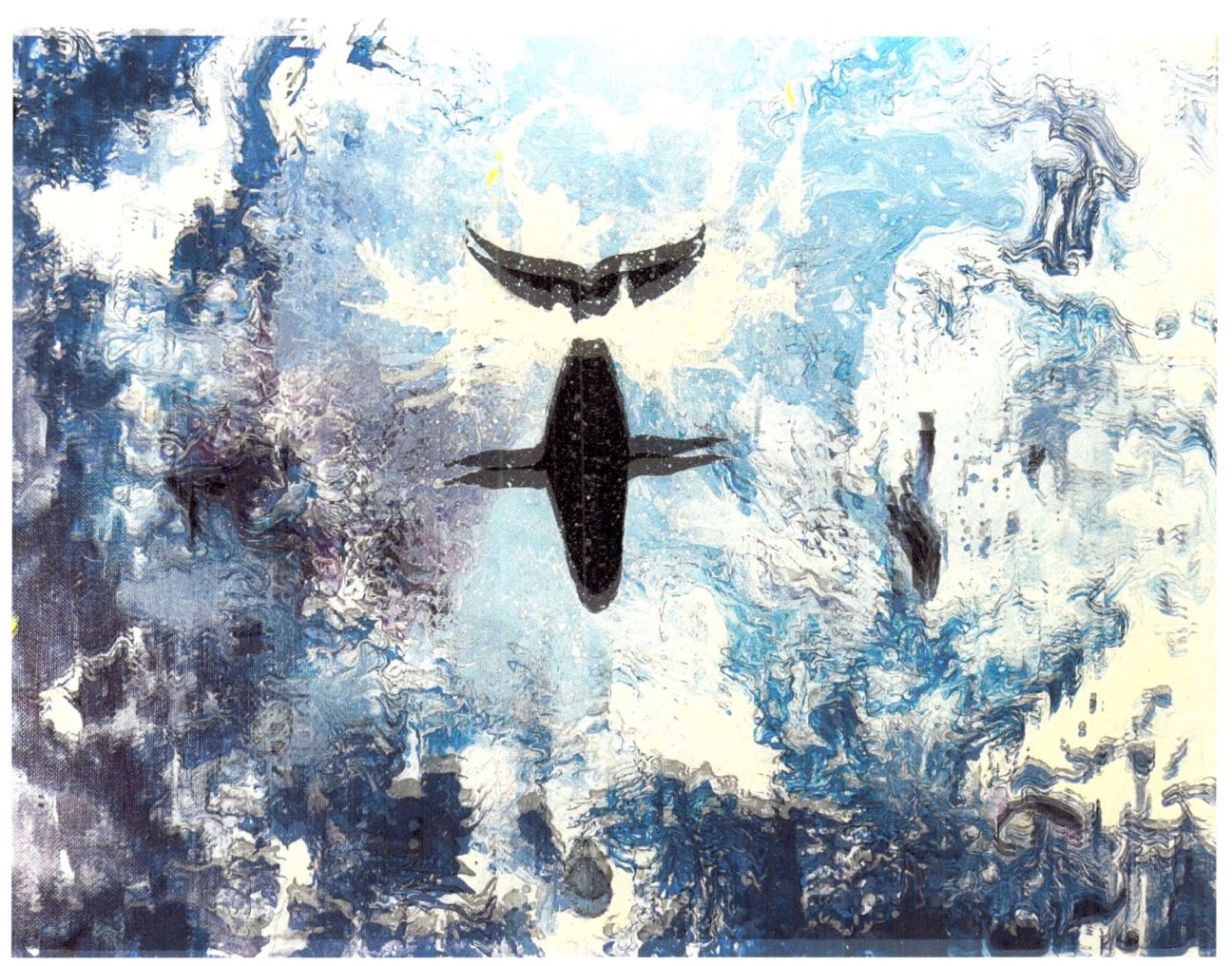

www.ingramcontent.com/pod-product-compliance
Lightning Source LLC
Chambersburg PA
CBHW051951210526
45473CB00023B/924